Japanese Cookery

THE AUTHORS

Margaret Leeming, who lives near Leeds with her husband and family, is a cookery writer with a special interest in the origins and history of food and cooking styles. Her most recent book, with co-author May Huang Man-hui, is *Chinese Regional Cookery* (also in the Rider series), and she has also broadcast on cookery topics for Radio Leeds.

Mutsuko Kohsaka lives with her family just outside Tokyo, where she trained in domestic science. She maintains a strong interest in European as well as Japanese cookery, and it was the mutual interest of the two authors in the cuisines of their respective countries that brought about their co-authorship of this book.

Also by Margaret Leeming

Chinese Cooking, with May Huang Man-hui
French Family Cooking
Chinese Regional Cookery, with May Huang Man-hui

Japanese Cookery

Margaret Leeming &
Mutsuko Kohsaka

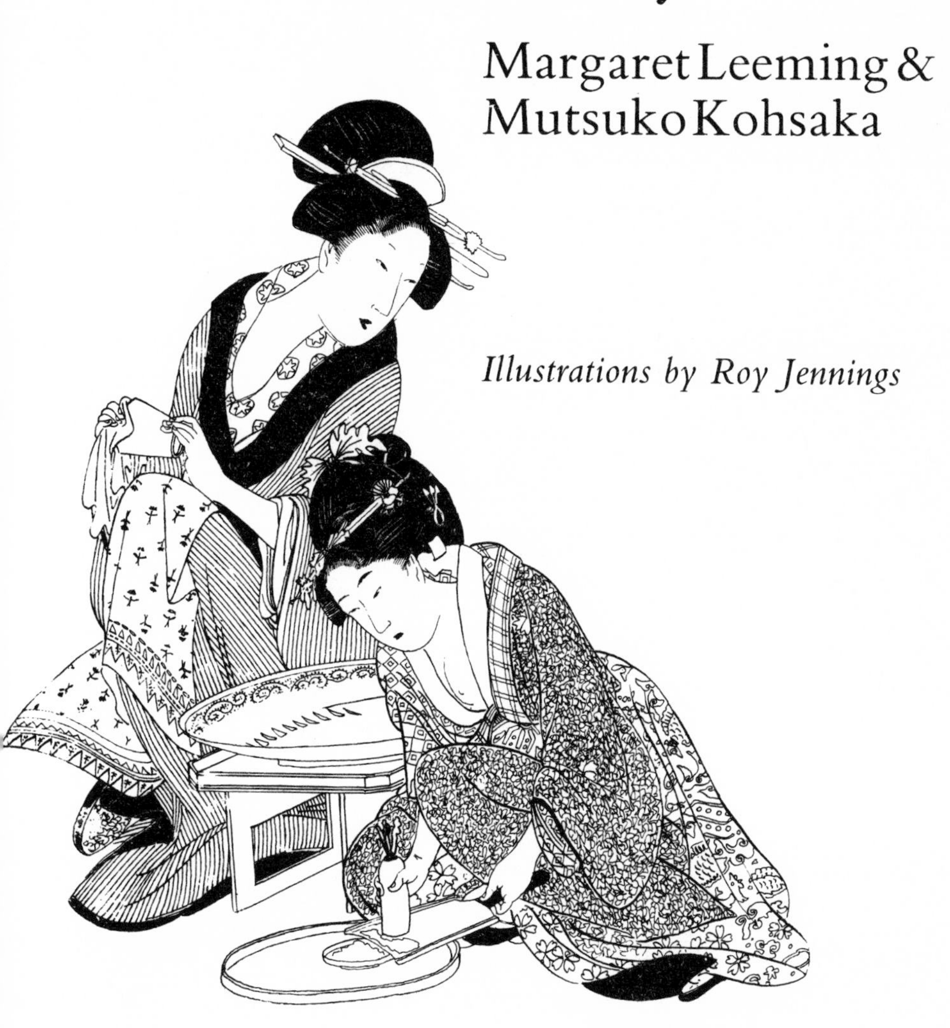

Illustrations by Roy Jennings

Rider
London Melbourne Sydney Auckland Johannesburg

Rider and Company Ltd
An imprint of the Hutchinson Publishing Group
17–21 Conway Street London W1P 6JD

Hutchinson Group (Australia) Pty Ltd
30–32 Cremorne Street, Richmond South, Victoria 3121
PO Box 151, Broadway, New South Wales 2007

Hutchinson Group (NZ) Ltd
32–34 View Road, PO Box 40–086, Glenfield, Auckland 10

Hutchinson Group (SA) (Pty) Ltd
PO Box 337, Bergvlei 2012, South Africa

First published 1984

Set in Linotron Bembo by
Wyvern Typesetting Ltd, Bristol

Printed and bound in Great Britain by
Anchor Brendon Limited, Tiptree, Essex

ISBN 0 09 154801 2

For Mary
Alice
Richard
Anna
Eiji
Shinji

Chapter decorations (re-drawn by Roy Jennings from Japanese originals): Grating white radish (Edo), page 3; rice cake shop on the Tokaido road (Edo), page 9; fish porters (Edo), page 19; kitchen scene (thirteenth century), page 27; cutting *sashimi* (Edo), page 42; making beancurd (Edo), page 83; picking pears (Edo), page 109; wayside tea-house (Edo), page 129; *soba* stall (Edo), page 142; travellers eating at an inn (Edo), page 156; Nihombashi Bridge (the Great Bridge of Japan), Tokyo (Edo), page 164.

Practical illustrations:
flower cutting, page 28; drop lid and saucepan, page 30; place setting, page 39; preparation of fish, page 43; skewering fish, pages 44–5; two ways of cutting *sashimi*, page 46; use of rolling mat, page 74; beancurd box, page 97.

Contents

Food in Japanese culture

The Japanese do not find it easy to introduce their homeland to the West. Theirs is a country in which the geisha girl and the tea ceremony co-exist with intensive, and intensely progressive, industrialization. Traditional and modern, old and new, are simply two facets of Japan's complex society – a society which has the wisdom to value the best of both.

Food, for the most part, remains traditional. Restrained in quantity, excellent in quality and elegant in presentation, Japanese meals are a world apart from the Western diner's overloaded dinner-plate. Yet the Japanese style of eating, which is dependent on fresh ingredients, emphasizes natural flavours and incorporates no animal fat (nor very much meat), could foster a new approach to eating in the diet-conscious, health-seeking West. The appeal of Japanese food also stems from the painstaking care taken in the treatment of each ingredient – the antithesis of the fast-food syndrome: in eel restaurants chefs still grill the fresh eels over huge charcoal braziers, positioning the skewered fish along the troughs of glowing charcoal, painting them with sweetened soy sauce and flicking over the skewers in rhythmic perpetual motion; chefs in the *sushi* bars, still wearing the traditional spotted headband of the Japanese workman, cut the raw fish with lightning speed and the precision born of long experience.

Again, the traditional and the modern stand side by side, however, for it is all too likely that hamburgers, beefburgers, milkshakes and ice-cream sodas will be on sale on the same street as the *sushi* bar, the eel restaurant or the noodle-house.

Japan combines tremendous style and sophistication with the garish, great beauty with the downright ugly. An exquisite flower arrangement may be found in a public lavatory under a flyover; the featureless concrete mass of a big city lies but a few miles away from breathtaking mountain and forest scenery. Such contrasts are echoed in Japan's physical characteristics: the climate ranges from sub-tropical in Kyushu to temperate in Hokkaido, where the winter snows last for four months. Three-quarters of the land in Japan is mountainous, forested and virtually empty, whilst two-thirds of the people squeeze together in the coastal plains and river valleys. If the Japanese islands were laid upon a map of Europe, Japan would stretch from Munich to the Outer Hebrides, with Tokyo lying over London. Yet in area Japan is only two-thirds the size of France, while her population (117 million) equals that of Britain and France together.. Isolated both from the West by her geographical position and from Asia by her westernized economic and industrial success, she belongs now to neither world, but stands alone in both.

Many Japanese see their country as having two aspects, an old-fashioned, traditional Chinese side centred on Kyoto and the west, and the *samurai*-based, money-conscious society of Tokyo and the east, where there are far fewer overt links with the past. By Asian standards Japan does not have a long history, since very little is known of the people who lived in the Japanese islands before the time of Christ. It is generally accepted that before 2000 BC a hunting and fishing people migrated from Central Asia through Korea to western and central Honshu, the largest island of Japan. At a much later date, somewhere around 250 BC, another group of people, also of Central Asian origin, arrived in Kyushu, the southern island of Japan, from Korea. These people were farmers, who at some stage in their migration had learnt the art of growing rice in paddy-fields.

Throughout Japanese history there has been only one imperial dynasty, which originated, it was said, in the struggles between the gods of sun and storm. In terms of historical fact, one family emerged as the dominant clan in the early centuries of the first millennium AD and probably associated themselves with these legendary struggles to strengthen their position among the other clans.

During these early centuries Japan had no written language and much of what is known of her history and her people's way of life comes from Chinese and Korean records. An account of Japan written in Chinese in the third century reveals that 'in winter as in summer the people live on vegetables. They serve their food on bamboo or wooden trays, eating with their fingers' (the Chinese at this time were already using chopsticks). It was also recorded that a Japanese embassy had visited the capital of China in AD 57, which resulted in Chinese scribes being employed at the Japanese imperial court from that time onwards. Chinese influence on Japan became increasingly strong, reaching Japan mainly through Korea, Japan's closest neighbour on the Asian mainland, for at this time northern Korea was a Chinese province and many Chinese had settled in south Korea. It has been estimated that by the sixth century 100,000 Koreans and Chinese were settled in Japan. They were skilled craftsmen and would certainly have been better educated than the indigenous people.

Inevitably these settlers introduced, among other aspects of their culture, Chinese food and eating habits, including the use of chopsticks. They sat on mats on the floor to eat their meals, as is still the custom in Japan today, although flat cushions are used instead of the mats. In China at that time a man's wealth could partly be calculated in the number of his jars of fermented bean-paste (a form of *miso*), and recipes for making both this and soy sauce date from the sixth century. Today soy sauce is a prominent feature of both Chinese and Japanese cookery, but only Japan retains *miso* as a basic ingredient in her cuisine. Another sixth-century Chinese recipe which has survived only in Japan is this recipe for *sushi*:

> Take a big carp, but not too fat. Clean and sprinkle with salt and leave to drain. Test to see if there is enough salt. Cook the rice. Put shredded orange peel and wine in a basket [*sic*] and mix together. Layer the fish and rice alternately with the lean at the bottom and the fat at the top. If red water comes out, throw it away. Wait until white juice comes and it tastes sour, then eat it.

This recipe is almost the same as that for *nare-sushi*, which was still being made in this way until very recently in the west of Japan.

Another recipe from the same Chinese source, closely resembling modern Japanese *yakimono*, is for grilled meats:

> Cut any kind of meat into small cubes and marinate with crushed onions, salt and soy sauce. Then thread on skewers and roast over a fire, turning frequently. Eat hot.

It was not until the twelfth century, however, that spit-roasting became one of the foremost cooking styles in Japanese cuisine, as it remains to this day.

The Chinese by the sixth century were seasoning their foods with sesame seeds, ginger, vinegar and sour plums – all seasonings that are in general use in Japan today. White radish was often used as a seasoning in China during these early centuries, instead of pepper or ginger. This practice survives in Japan though it is now rare in China.

Noodles had been eaten by everyone in China, including the court and nobility, for three hundred years before the sixth century. It is difficult not to believe that all these foods and cooking methods, in constant use in modern Japan, were known at least to some degree in Japan by the sixth century.

In the seventh and eighth centuries contact with China became steadily closer. Buddhism, already the official religion of the court in China, was introduced and adopted by the ruling Japanese families, alongside the indigenous Shinto religion. Buddhist monks for a long period enjoyed a monopoly of learning in Japan, and contact between monasteries in Japan, China and Korea was continuous. The coming of Buddhism to Japan inevitably had a great influence on the food habits of the people. As Buddhism forbids the killing of any animal for food all practising Buddhists are vegetarians. So in Japan during the seventh and eighth centuries an increasing number of monks and lay people including the nobility became vegetarians. Beancurd (*tofu*), a vegetable protein, was an ingredient in a Chinese recipe written in the seventh century, although it was probably known much earlier. It was almost certainly introduced to Japan at this time, while the Japanese themselves invented *natto* (fermented whole soya beans) at some time during the eighth century. The Japanese nobility had an ambivalent attitude to some Buddhist precepts, for they interpreted the prohibition on taking life as applying only to four-legged animals. They continued to eat fish, and to hunt for birds and game – calling wild boar 'mountain whale' to excuse their killing. The peasants on the other hand had little opportunity to eat any foods other than vegetables and grain; one surviving description of a meal for carpenters working at the imperial palace in the tenth century mentions only soup, vegetables and rice.

At this time Chinese written characters were fitted to the Japanese spoken language so that records could be kept and Buddhist *sutras* (holy texts) read. The writings of Confucius and the Chinese Legalists were introduced and their theories concerning absolutism and the ranking of classes became one of the foundations of Japanese society. Japanese official parties of up to 500 people at a time visited Ch'ang-an – the capital of China, near modern Xian – and were tremendously impressed by the vigour and grandeur of the Chinese court.

Nara and later Heian (Kyoto) were established as capital cities in imitation of Ch'ang-an. The Japanese in the seventh century were stimulated by a desire to imitate and adapt for themselves whatever they admired in Chinese culture. This desire to emulate has continued throughout their history to the present day, when there is hardly any aspect of Japanese life, from food and clothes through literature to industrial technology, which does not demonstrate the capacity of the

Japanese to adapt and re-mould for their own community whatever they admire in others.

By the end of the ninth century all official contacts with the Chinese court had ended, although many Japanese monks, students and merchants still travelled privately to China. The first great flush of enthusiasm for Chinese things was over, and for nearly 500 years the Japanese concentrated on absorbing the Chinese culture to which they had already been exposed, rather than on extending it. It was during this time that the foundations of the courtly style of Japanese cooking were established, mirroring the ceremonial life of the imperial court at Kyoto, and that Japan became a feudal state with great land-owning families, or clans, holding power through their estates. The *samurai* emerged as the gentry class, owners of these estates, but they in turn swore total loyalty to an overlord who gave them his protection. During this period there was almost continuous civil war throughout Japan. The emperors became ciphers and the country was ruled by regents, later called *Shōguns*.

In stark contrast to the impoverishment of the countryside, and despite the devastation caused by warfare and the effects of high taxation, indigenous Japanese art and culture, albeit still deeply influenced by Chinese ideals, prospered during this period. Poetry, painting, sculpture and flower-arranging reached a peak of excellence during the fourteenth century, influenced mainly by the court but also by the renewed vigour of Buddhist philosophy. Cultural ties with China were at length re-established despite the political chaos, and through trade with China came the beginnings of prosperity in Japan. The growth of *samurai* power brought a change to the food and lifestyles of the gentry in Japan, and a plainer, 'military' style of cooking evolved. The development of Zen Buddhism aroused an interest in natural beauty and an intellectual approach to nature. During the fourteenth and fifteenth centuries Japanese style and intellectualism were both greatly stimulated by the work of artists under the patronage of the *Shōguns* in Kyoto. It was under the guidance of these artists that the tea ceremony, some elements of which had been current in China 700 years previously, was developed and formalized by the *Shōguns* and the court. Influenced by early Zen beliefs in restraint and simplicity, the tea ceremony took the form of a meeting of a group of friends at which strict rules of formal behaviour were observed. The ceremony would be held in a quiet and aesthetically pleasing place, and as well as drinking tea, served by the 'tea master', the participants would discuss and admire beauty – in nature, in art objects, or in the simple utensils of the tea ceremony. The formal ritual of the tea-making promoted discipline and restraint within the group taking part, and to this day both men and women find relaxation and serenity in this ancient custom. To have attended classes and become a tea master (male or female) is the mark of a traditionally well-educated Japanese, and today there is a growing trend among Japanese girls to take tea-ceremony classes preparatory to marriage.

During the second half of the sixteenth century Japan was ruled successively by three very powerful military *Shōguns*, under whose rules peace was established. This new stability provided a basis for the great cultural flowering of the Edo period (1615–1854).

It was during the reign of the first of these *Shōguns* that the first Europeans landed in Japan. They were three Portuguese traders, blown off their route by a storm in about 1542, and it seems that they were well received by the Japanese. Within a few years many Spanish and Portuguese, mainly merchants and Jesuit and Dominican missionaries (including St Francis Xavier), landed in Japan. By the early seventeenth century Dutch and English traders had also arrived, bringing with them the quarrels – over trade, land and religion – that at that time were causing so much turmoil in Europe. The rivalry and dissension between the Europeans existed not only in the Catholic/Protestant schism, but in political and commercial struggles between the Spanish and Portuguese, between the Spanish and Dutch and the Spanish and the English; inevitably the Japanese converts of the European missionaries inherited their attitudes to other European factions. In general, the Japanese treated the foreigners with courtesy and tolerance, and were fascinated by their habits, possessions and knowledge.

So, indeed, were the Europeans by all they saw in Japan – not least by the food. An Elizabethan account of 'the Kingdome of Japania' includes a description of it:

> Fish, rootes and rice are their common junkets, and if they chance to kill a hen, ducke or pigge, which is but seldome, they will not like churles eat it alone, but their friends shall be surely partakers of it . . . . They have the same kyndes of beastes that we have both tame and wilde, but they seldome eat anye fleshe, but that which is taken with huntinge. Indeed they delight not much in fleshe, but they live for the most part with hearbes, fyshe, barley and ryce: which things are their chieffe nuwrishments. Their ordinary drink is water, and that is made most times hot in the same pot where they seeth their ryce, that so it may receive some thickness and substance from the ryce. They have strong wine and rack distilled of ryce, of which they will sometimes drink largely . . . . As concerning another drinke, they take great delighte in water mingled with a certain powder which is very pretiouse, which they call *chai* [tea].

It seems probable that the Europeans – perhaps the Portuguese – introduced the idea of flour and egg batters to the Japanese. European cookbooks dating from the early fifteenth century onwards include recipes for such batters, for making both savoury and sweet fritters. By the early sixteenth century European cooks had discovered how to use eggs as a raising agent in cakes, and it is likely that the Japanese developed both *tempura* (foods fried in batter) and *kasutera* (a form of sponge cake) as a result of their European contacts. (The word *kasutera* is from Castella – or Castille – in Spain.) Tobacco and sweet potatoes, both American in origin, were introduced to Japan by the Spanish or Dutch, probably through the Philippines.

However, the excessive crusading zeal of the Portuguese and Spanish missionaries and the open quarrels between the religious orders, together with the fear that their presence might eventually lead to European conquest of Japan, resulted, first, in the banning of the missionaries, then in the suppression of Christianity, and finally in the closing of Japan to all outsiders. The Japanese themselves were forbidden to leave the country, and the building of any ship capable of sailing on the open sea was prohibited.

The only contacts with the outside world that the Japanese maintained were with a small Dutch settlement on an island in Nagasaki harbour, where two calls per year by a trading ship were permitted, and with a very strictly controlled Chinese ghetto, also in Nagasaki. In return for these privileges the Dutch were required to visit Edo (Tokyo) annually and report on Western political and scientific developments.

In 1692 a Dutch physician named Englebert Kaemphfer kept a diary of his journey to Edo in which the following account of Japanese food appears:

> There were numerous tea-shops and cookshops where were sold mansje [*manju*], a sort of round cake which they learnt to make from the Portuguese [more probably *manju* are Chinese in origin]; they were as big as common hens' eggs and sometimes filled within with black-bean flower [flour] and sugar; cakes of the jelly of the Kaads root [*konnyaku*?], which root is found upon mountains and cut into round slices like carrots and roasted [possibly there is a confusion here between mountain yams and the sub-species of the sweet potato *Amorphalus konjac*, used to make *konnyaku*], snails, shellfish and other small fish roasted, boiled or pickled; Chinese laxa [noodles?] is a thin sort of pap, or paste, made of fine wheat flower cut into small thin long slices and baked; all sorts of plants, roots and sprigs which the season affords washed and cleaned and then boiled in water with salt; . . . the common sauce for these and other dishes is a little Soje [soy sauce] as they call it, mixed with sakki [*sake*] or the beer of the country. Sansjo [*sansho*] leaves are laid upon the dish for ornament's sake, and sometimes thin slices of fine ginger and lemon peel.

He reports that the Japanese traveller ate three times a day: before daybreak he had a substantial breakfast, at noon he ate dinner and he ended the day with a good supper.

Kaemphfer also described several dinners or 'treats' that he was given in the houses of various officials at Edo. One included 'tea, tobacco, philosophical or white syrup [sic], steen-brassen [*tai*, or sea bream], a very scarce fish, boiled in a brown sauce. Another dish of fish dressed with beanflower [*miso*] and spices. Cakes of eggs rolled together, and fried fish which were presented to us on green skewers of bambous [sic]. Lemon peels with sugar.' At another meal they were given 'two long slices of mange [gourd] dipped into a brown sup or sauce, with some ginger. Hard eggs. Four common fish fried and brought in on skewers of bamboo. The stomachs of carps salted [salted roes] in a brown sauce. Two small slices of a goose roasted and warm, presented in unglazed earthern dishes.'

They had no rice at either of these meals, Kaemphfer observed, but plenty of *sake*, as in the first part of a modern Japanese meal.

For the 250 years of the Edo period Japan remained a closed society, in which all aspects of life developed in a unique and completely Japanese manner. Initially the *Shōguns* were extremely powerful. They established a new capital city of Edo (Tokyo) while the imperial court remained isolated in Kyoto. They forced the great land-owning nobility to spend the greater part of each year at Edo. They defined the *samurai* class, no longer small land-owners but hereditary professional soldiers, living in towns and owing allegiance to an overlord who paid them in measures of rice. The great land-owning nobles themselves collected their rents in measures of rice, but with the increasing urbanization of the aristocracy money took the place of rice as currency and a new class of wealthy urban merchants grew up to convert the rice incomes of the nobility into cash.

These newly rich families, often originally rice or *sake* merchants, wanted the refinements of life that wealth could provide. They created a new demand for the work of skilled craftsmen. A style and taste developed that were truly Japanese, and luxuries were enjoyed by a greater section of the community than ever before, despite continual efforts by the government to curb the extravagant lifestyle of the merchants. There were perceptible differences in taste between Kyoto, influenced by the imperial court and remaining more Chinese, restrained and traditional, and Edo, where the style, influenced by the military aristocracy and the newly rich bourgeoisie, became more Japanese, freer and more vigorous.

The life of the farmer during Edo times in Japan was extremely hard. For the most part he was regarded merely as a producer of rice to support the urban community, particularly the aristocracy. Various government edicts referred to the farmers as people without sense or forethought who should have just enough food to keep themselves alive and no more. In 1694 they were ordered to rise early, work at night, not to eat rice but to be content with coarser foods and to abstain from tea and tobacco. Throughout the Edo period they were forbidden to eat white rice. Yet more disadvantaged than the farmers during Edo times were the outcasts or non-humans. Some of these were temporary outcasts through some misdeed or misfortune but others belonged to the hereditary caste which handled dead animals and worked with leather. These people, who were bound by law always to follow what to the Japanese was a shameful profession, and to live in segregated districts or villages, were forbidden to conceal their origins. (Their hereditary legal disabilities were removed in 1871 but the social constraints upon them continued until after the Second World War.)

In the mid-nineteenth century the barriers broke. The economic stresses which had built up in Japan during the gradual change from a feudal rice economy to a commercial economy were paralleled by increasing pressure from Western mercantile powers for permission to trade. The Japanese seclusion ended and at almost the same time (1868) the Meiji emperor took over the government from the Shōgunate. One of the very first visitors to Japan after the ending of the seclusion has left a description of a street scene in Nagasaki:

> In one part a confectioner's shop . . . [with] sweetmeats, . . . rice dumplings and rye cakes. . . . In another part a fishmonger's stall covered with conger eels, mackerel, soles, lobsters and crayfish, or with sliced cutlets of star fish and cuttle fish. . . . Occasionally a butcher's shambles . . . where a whale lately stranded on a neighbouring beach or harpooned by an adventurous fleet of fishing boats furnished an over-abundant and cheap supply of coarse red meat resembling raw beef.

Under the direction of the Meiji emperor, Japan embraced the new world of the West, reshaped her constitution, created new industries and a new army and navy modelled on European patterns. New, mainly European, habits of food and cooking were introduced. Bread and beer became a standard part of Japanese life. Before the Meiji reforms very little meat was eaten in Japan, even by the rich. Domestic poultry was kept mainly for eggs, though a few chickens were eaten – particularly very young chickens, eaten raw as *sashimi*. Game such as duck, deer and wild boar (the nobility loved hunting) featured on the menus of the wealthy. With the Meiji reforms, pork became an accepted food: breaded pork cutlets, similar to the European *Schnitzel*, became popular (these were deep-fried, rather than shallow-fried as in the West). During Edo times the killing of oxen for food had been explicitly forbidden, and indeed with the possible exception of a small area around Nagasaki beef was an unknown food in Japan. Now, with the emphasis on Western eating habits, beef slowly became an acceptable food item, although it was not until the twentieth century that it became really popular. The Japanese evolved a style of their own for cooking beef (*sukiyaki*), together with various folk-tales explaining its origins.

However, since the last decades of the nineteenth century and to varying degrees during the twentieth there has been a new dimension to the relationship between Japan and the West. Japan is no longer a recipient only: it has become an originator of ideas. Many European artists, including Toulouse-Lautrec and the potter Bernard Leach, have found inspiration in the forms and style of both popular and traditional Japanese art. Modern Western design owes a great deal to Japanese artists. But Japanese influences in the West extend beyond the arts. The great master of *nouvelle cuisine*, Bocuse, says he learnt as much as he taught in Japan. Certainly in the presentation of food *nouvelle cuisine* appears to have been greatly influenced by traditional Japanese forms. Japanese influence is also to be found in the emphasis now placed on the freshness and natural flavours of food, and in the greater freedom and confidence that are exercised in exploring and developing them. A delicacy and lightness have replaced the rich coating sauces of French *haute cuisine*.

In today's world, with its fast communication systems and the almost instant interchange of food fashions, Japan takes a leading part in both receiving and passing on food habits. Once so heavily dependent on outside influences, Japanese cookery now has a clear national identity of its own – an identity which, it is hoped, will be retained alongside its future acquisitions.

Japanese food and society today

The outward face of Japan was transformed from 1868, the beginning of the Meiji era, onwards by the political, military and economic reforms which were designed to turn her into a Western nation, and yet her traditions remain Confucian even today, and in some ways pre-Confucian. The Japanese people themselves live with a split personality, deeply traditional in their attitude towards society and in their reverence for the family while effortlessly adapting to the latest industrial technology in their work. They insist that their country is poor, while they enjoy considerable material riches gained by their work – Japan has the third largest economy in the world, and living standards are now European, if not American. Western people often find it hard to understand Japanese outlooks, and likewise many Japanese find Western attitudes equally incomprehensible.

Like other Asian societies, Japanese society is comprised of a series of groups. Every individual belongs to at least one group, in which each accepts his own role and status and makes his relationships accordingly. A group is the family, or the firm for which one works, or a university where membership is almost like a club, or a combination of these. Within the groups there are strict codes of formal and informal behaviour and language, including different language forms for speaking to those of different rank, even from father to son and son to father. Society runs smoothly as long as no one breaks these codes of social behaviour, and there is continual pressure for everyone to conform. 'We believe that everyone should be the same,' said a Japanese politician visiting the West recently; Japanese society has no place for individualists or misfits. Foreigners have no place in Japanese society, and no position in any group; for this reason special codes and rules have to be made to accommodate them. Difficulty of communication itself, in a wider sense than mere language, contributes to the mystery of Japan.

Obedience to the rules of behaviour is seen by most Japanese people as an insurance that guarantees protection by the group, for an individual without a group has few prospects either economically or socially. But these groups are sexist: women have no place in men's groups, nor men in women's. The groups draw a clear distinction between men's and women's work. This works against women in two ways: it prevents them from holding almost all administrative jobs, since these are classed as men's jobs, and by defining women's work as second-class, it ties women to unimportant jobs; as a result most women are forced to take lower-paid work. Most Japanese men consider that they cannot retain their self-respect if they help their wives in the kitchen, even in the privacy of their own homes, whatever full-time job she may also have. Married women complain that one of the most serious disadvantages in their lives is the lack of genuine sharing between them and their husbands. A wife is expected to obey her husband without discussion, and if she is with him in public she will generally remain silent.

Marriages in Japan are arranged, as they are in most Asian communities. Either partner has the right to refuse, but the basic arrangement for the majority of marriages is a business contract between the two families drawn up with the help of a marriage broker, rather than an emotional relationship, as in the West. The pressures from society make it almost impossible for a woman not to marry and have children. Eldest sons are still expected to live in their father's house after they are married. This leads to serious problems between the mother and the daughter-in-law; in fact many girls refuse to marry eldest sons. The bond between mothers and sons is particularly strong in Japan; the bond between husband and wife is often much weaker, and a new wife is extremely vulnerable. She is expected by tradition to shop, cook and care for her parents-in-law, whatever other commitments she may have with babies or a job. The stress of sharing a kitchen with an unsympathetic older woman can lead to a great deal of unhappiness. However, within her own family a married woman does have power, partly through her influence over her son, partly by virtue of her eventual position as a mother-in-law, partly because she controls the family finances. She traditionally receives her husband's pay packet, and although she must pay his bills without question she can, if she is careful and frugal, save money for herself.

Away from the big industrial centres many men are forced to migrate to the towns to find work, at least for part of the year. This leaves the women in these areas to run the small-scale businesses, such as farms and local retail outlets, themselves; in the urban areas widows often run their own small businesses, such as bars, shops or even wholesale companies. Freedom and power for women are achieved through economic independence; but since the position of women is so closely bound into the economic structure of Japan, social change is very slow.

A different picture is suggested by Japanese food and eating habits. Here in the last forty years change has been very rapid. The Japanese today are very proud of their diet. As a Japanese friend explained, 'There are three grades of eating. The lowest keeps you alive, the next gives you pleasure, whilst the highest not only does these, but is good for you as well. We in Japan have achieved this grade with our food.' It is interesting to compare this contemporary view of eating with that of a villager some fifty years ago, who said that eating was not a matter of any importance but a necessity for sustaining life, and therefore should be as brief a business as possible. During the first half of this century it was the policy of the Japanese government to encourage the people in abstinence and attitudes of poverty towards all material things including food. This philosophy, together with the experience of semi-starvation at the end of the Second World War, has left a mark on most Japanese over 35 years old. They are still conditioned to a habit of careful economy where food is concerned. Nevertheless they now take great pleasure in the abundance of foods available.

The average family in the 1920s, and indeed for the following thirty years, lived on rice – about 0.4 kg (1 lb) per day per person – together with bean products such as beancurd and *miso*, pickles, vegetables, a little fish and an occasional egg. Nowadays families expect to eat fish or some kind of seafood every day, and meat, such as chicken, every week if not every day. Buddhist vegetarian beliefs are no longer a strong influence in the community as a whole, although many homes still maintain a Buddhist shrine in the living room. However, many older people choose to eat meat only rarely – a clear division between the generations.

Because vegetables are associated with the poverty diets of previous generations, some Japanese families are unwilling to eat them in any quantity. Yet unlike the vegetables available to the poorer, peasant communities in the Far East, the vegetables sold in Japan are of an outstanding quality, flawless in shape and condition.

The main characteristics of modern Japanese food are the freshness of the flavours and the delicacy of the seasonings. After eating Japanese food for a time, the Western visitor to Japan is able to distinguish subtle degrees of natural flavour in the foods that would be hidden and overlaid by more highly seasoned foods. The Buddhist tradition is probably responsible for the absence, even today, of any quantity of onions, garlic or coriander (the latter almost unknown in Japan) in Japanese cooking. These were considered 'rank' flavours and were consequently forbidden by Buddhist dietary rules. The main seasoning elements used are soy sauce, generally lighter and saltier than the Chinese soy sauces to which we have become accustomed in the West; *sake* or rice wine, which removes strong flavours and lifts delicate ones; rice vinegar, which is gentle, appetizing and without any of the harshness often found in Western vinegars; and sugar, which gives an impressive lift to many savoury dishes. In the home, sugar is used almost exclusively as a condiment, like salt; cakes and desserts are never made at home. The quantity of sugar bought by Japanese households is approximately one-quarter of that purchased by similar-sized families in the UK. Although no Japanese housewife would consider making cakes herself, it is customary to buy small sweet cakes to eat as a snack between meals (often in the middle of the afternoon). These are sometimes Western-style small cakes of exquisite appearance, sometimes traditional Japanese cakes of a jelly-like texture – small works of art in shining greens, mauves and yellows – and sometimes cakes made from glutinous rice flour and stuffed with red-bean paste.

The Japanese eat very little animal fat or poly-unsaturated oils; their dairy industry operates on a very limited scale. The fat in their diet comes from oily fish such as mackerel and salmon and from dishes such as *tempura* and *tonkatsu* which are fried in vegetable oil.

The Japanese start the day with a large breakfast. This traditionally includes a large bowl of hot rice eaten with some form of relish, such as a raw egg stirred into it or fermented soya beans (*natto*), together with a few sheets of *nori* seaweed, some lightly pickled vegetables and a *miso* soup with beancurd and seaweed or vegetables. Sometimes there is a portion of salted fish, and always there is green tea. Most people at work eat lunch away from home, sometimes from luncheon boxes filled with cold rice and pickles, otherwise at small restaurants serving noodles or rice dishes. The main meal of the day, whether eaten in a restaurant or at home, is the evening meal. This is always a hot, cooked meal: at its simplest rice, pickles and *miso* soup, with green tea to drink, but usually including several different dishes of fish and vegetables, one of which would probably be dressed with vinegar as a salad, together with the soup and rice.

A major difference between those families that retain traditional eating habits and the so-called 'modern' families exists in the use of bread – usually sliced, factory-made bread. A traditional family eats a Japanese breakfast, the preparation of which demands a considerable amount of time and effort. As a result many Japanese families today prefer to eat a Western breakfast of bread or toast together with a salad, ham and pickles. Some modern families even eat bread with their midday meal instead of rice; however, at the main meal in the evening everyone always eats rice.

Eating bread with Japanese food is not a new idea: in 1890 it was reported that there were piles of loaves on every little cook-stall in Tokyo, and for a while it was all the rage. The Japanese have always been willing to try out new foods and eating styles, and this no doubt explains the popularity of foreign food products and restaurants.

In contemporary Japanese food there is little regional variation. Certain pickles have regional connections, but they can usually be bought elsewhere in Japan. *Miso* is still made at home by some traditional families, where every woman member joins in the boiling and grinding of the beans. Families have their own recipes and sometimes their own special supply of soya beans grown in a particular area, and therefore a certain regional quality is retained. Some other dishes, too, are associated with particular areas or styles of cooking, although they may now be found everywhere in Japan. Their origins are often indicated in the form 'Kyoto-style' or 'Nagasaki-style', the latter particularly associated with meat dishes. The 'Kyoto style' of cooking is the traditional cooking of the court dating from the ninth century, while 'Kanto-' (or eastern-) style cooking developed during the thirteenth century from the spartan lifestyle of the *samurai*. It is closely associated with the tea ceremony, which derived from Zen Buddhist philosophy. The latter influences the choice of foods, dictating that their natural forms should be retained and that they should be used in their proper season; rules for the colour and appearance of the finished dishes are also stipulated. Zen philosophy still influences the formal *haute cuisine* of all Japanese banquets.

Perhaps the clearest regional variation still maintained between the east and west of Japan is in the soup that accompanies noodles. The soup eaten in Tokyo and the east is darker and heavier than the soup from Kyoto and the west, partly because in the west a light soy sauce is used in much of the cooking.

Everybody in Japan eats noodles – not the yellow egg noodles familiar in the West and associated with Italy, but fine white noodles with a clean, fresh taste, made from wheat flour and called *udon*. These are especially popular in the west of Japan, while in the north and in

Tokyo greyish-coloured noodles called *soba*, made from buckwheat flour, are more popular. So high is the reputation of certain chefs for their fresh noodles that people go out of their way to be able to eat that particular kind. (There are often references in Japanese literature to eating *soba* or *udon* at some famous noodle-house.)

There are noodle-houses everywhere in Japan, many of them very small. They usually serve only noodles, and are rather spartan, but can be relied upon for a quick, cheap meal. At lunch-time they are often crowded, with a queue of people waiting for seats. Once seated, customers devote themselves to eating rather than to conversation.

Other cheap restaurants, in towns, serve such dishes as *tonkatsu* (pork cutlet) or one-pot rice dishes. Like the noodle-houses they are generally crowded at lunch-time.

The atmosphere of a traditional Japanese restaurant is very different from that of a 'fast-food' house, although here too it may be necessary to queue for up to an hour for a table. Many of the more expensive restaurants serve only customers who have booked in advance, mainly because of the enormous amount of time and labour that goes into a Japanese restaurant meal. Each dish is made up of many meticulously prepared elements and in the final serving every dish for every diner has to be arranged individually. The dish when it appears often symbolizes an element in nature, such as autumn, rainfall or a cloud, and the diners at such a meal are expected to appreciate not just the taste of the food but also its aesthetic qualities. Menus at expensive restaurants are always limited and specialized, partly on account of the complexity of serving food at this standard and the continual demand for excellence, and also because of the Japanese view that exclusiveness is a desirable quality in itself. People go to a particular restaurant to eat a specific food or style of dish cooked to perfection. The average Japanese housewife does not try to compete with professional Japanese chefs; she is more likely to study French or Chinese cooking, since she has little incentive to reproduce the highly specialized dishes served in Japanese restaurants – nor would she be likely to possess the necessary equipment. Domestic cooking is therefore simpler than restaurant cooking, making use of a smaller range of ingredients and requiring less elaborate preparation. Many of the recipes that appear in this book belong to this category of Japanese cookery, and would be familiar to most Japanese housewives.

Almost all entertaining, especially business entertaining, of which there is a great deal in Japan, is done in restaurants. This practice is consistent with the Japanese attitude to women: a wife – 'the one within' – would be considered out of place at a business dinner, which is regarded as a strictly male affair. The custom of leaving the wife at home has encouraged the habit of taking home some portion of the meal for her in a 'doggy bag' – a standard feature of restaurant service.

Most restaurants have part of their dining area covered with traditional *tatami* mats. Firm but springy to walk on, these are made with layers of finely woven rice straw and smell, when new, of newly mown hay. The matting designates the area as 'traditional', and the Japanese never wear shoes when in traditional rooms, nor do they have chairs in them. The mats are on a raised floor area about a foot above the normal level. Diners shed their shoes before stepping on to the *tatami*, then kneel on flat cushions to eat at tables about 15 inches high. They kneel not in an upright position, as in church in the West, but resting back on the feet: this is called 'formal sitting'. Many people sit with their feet to one side of them in preference to kneeling, but this is not considered polite on formal occasions. The waitresses in restaurants slide off their shoes each time they step on to the *tatami*.

Sushi bars are another bastion of male exclusiveness in Japan, although there are a few 'women-only' bars in Tokyo. In these bars businessmen meet after office hours in an informal atmosphere to drink *sake* or beer and eat tiny mouthfuls of vinegared rice wrapped in *nori* (seaweed) and topped by thin slices of raw fish, or translucent apricot-coloured fish roe. On the other side of the bar chefs can be seen at work slicing the freshly killed fish, shaping and arranging the *sushi* into its traditional forms. Of course such skills and such ingredients (which must be extremely fresh) are not cheap, and few people can afford to make a meal of *sushi*. *Sushi* can also be ordered in advance and delivered to the home, where it arrives beautifully arranged on lacquer trays – a delight to the eye and an irresistible temptation to go on eating until no pieces are left. It is common practice to have a tray of *sushi* sent in as part of a special meal.

Providing meals at home is otherwise labour-intensive. The Japanese housewife expects to go shopping every day for the components of the evening meal. In the suburbs of every large town a wide variety of small local shops will be within easy reach. These shops – fishmongers, greengrocers, beancurd-makers, and so on – are usually family-run, and are typical of traditional small businesses in urban areas. However, problems over transport and wholesale marketing have increasingly prevented the shops from being able to obtain supplies of really fresh fish and vegetables. A recent survey of housewives' shopping habits showed that 70 per cent of housewives prefer to shop in supermarkets, where they can save time and money and where the goods are considered to be no less fresh than in the small shops. (Most Japanese families have refrigerators or fridge-freezers, almost a necessity in the hot summers, but most foods, including frozen foods, are bought only for immediate consumption.) Yet there is a growing feeling among many Japanese that to taste 'real' food one must go to the smaller towns, where farmers' wives still sell their produce direct to the consumer, as in French country markets.

In addition to sliced bread and pre-packed foods from the supermarket, the Japanese housewife also uses a range of other convenience foods, such as *teriyaki* sauce, instant soup stock and the very popular curry-mix, sold in varying strengths (all of them very bland). Many of these products now contain chemical additives to improve their performance, looks and keeping qualities. Some people consider that modern food in Japan is in danger of losing its essential quality of freshness, and is being overlaid with artificially created flavours. They fear that the younger generation will have no chance to distinguish between the two. At the same time foreign restaurants have become very popular, and they usually serve food which is more spicy than traditional Japanese food.

During the Edo period Japanese food had a strong national identity, and despite the Meiji reforms food and eating habits until the mid-twentieth century retained a distinctive Japanese quality, partly on account of the continuing poverty of the majority of the people. However, in the last twenty years material wealth, the media (especially television) and foreign package holidays have tended to encourage a growing consumer demand for new, 'fashionable' foods, which are usually foreign. The cultural confusion always present in Japan between that which is Asian and traditional and that which is Western and new is particularly marked in the field of food, where the traditional and indigenous seems steadily to be losing ground.

Getting started

All the methods of cooking used in Japanese cuisine are familiar to Western cooks and present no real problems. However, for some people the unfamiliar ingredients included in many Japanese recipes may pose a barrier to getting started. This chapter focuses on some everyday Japanese recipes which require few special ingredients but serve to illustrate Japan's different styles of cooking and are authentically Japanese. Using these recipes alone, it is possible to assemble two or three complete Japanese meals. A few of the more specialist garnishes and flavours that are such a feature of Japanese dishes are introduced, and advice on planning and serving Japanese meals can also be found at the end of the chapter.

One of the most important aspects of Japanese cooking is the quality of the original ingredients. It is impossible to recreate fresh flavours in foods which have already lost their taste through ageing or staling. Therefore in Japanese cooking the success of many recipes depends not just on the cooking but on the initial search for the freshest fish and vegetables. The Japanese aim at natural flavour above all else. To achieve this they cook with great delicacy, seasoning only to complement the foods, not to change them. Most Japanese dislike highly seasoned and particularly 'hot' foods, with the result that many Japanese dishes taste bland to Western palates conditioned to foreign food that is spicy. Extra and often rather intriguing seasonings are usually added to the food after it has been cooked in the form of dipping sauces – such as the piquant lemony *ponzu* sauce or a sweet-sour sauce based on sesame or walnuts. Garnishes such as *wasabi* mustard, which in flavour is half way between horseradish and English mustard, or a mildly peppery grated white radish and chilli, also contribute to the interest of the dish.

Almost all the equipment found in a Japanese kitchen would have its counterpart in the West. Moreover, it is perfectly possible to cook Japanese food without any special equipment. Curiously, despite the common origins of the Chinese and Japanese cuisines, the modern Japanese housewife does not use a *wok*. Most cooking is done in a saucepan or frying-pan.

Food is usually cut into small pieces for eating with chopsticks, generally before it is cooked, always before it is served. The pieces tend to be larger than those for Chinese dishes.

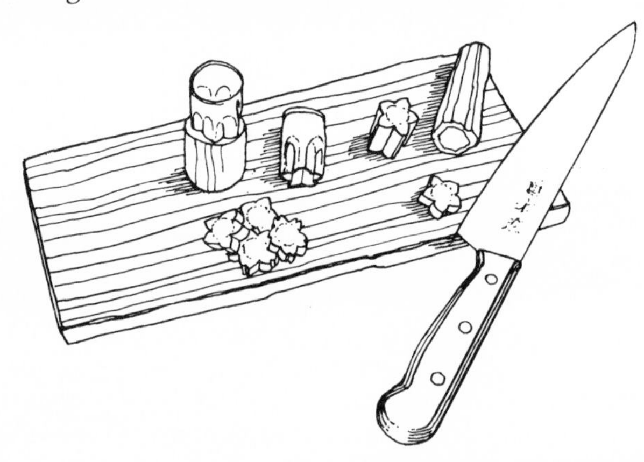

To begin with, there is no need to stock up on a vast number of esoteric ingredients for Japanese cooking: some dishes can be cooked using the contents of a Western store-cupboard with very few additions. The basics are soy sauce, fresh root ginger, rice vinegar (substitute diluted cider vinegar), *sake* (substitute diluted vodka), *mirin* (see below for substitute) and white sesame seeds. Once you have gained a little confidence, you may wish to add to these by acquiring, for example, some instant *dashi* (see below).

The Japanese generally use a light, salty soy sauce. Kikkoman is the trade name of the most commonly available brand in the West, but any *light* Chinese soy sauce may be substituted. Cider vinegar diluted to half strength with water may be used instead of rice vinegar. Vodka, diluted to half strength with an equal amount of water, is a good substitute for *sake* (Japanese rice wine): note that Western sherry has too strong and dominant a flavour. *Mirin* is a sweet, syrupy rice wine brewed by the Japanese only for cooking; it gives a fine glaze to grilled foods and creates a sweetness in sauces without being in the least sickly. A sugar-and-water syrup (half and half), or a sugar, water and vodka mixture (1 sugar, ½ water, ½ vodka) may be used instead, but *mirin* is best for an authentic Japanese flavour (Japanese and some Chinese shops stock it). Another very 'authentic' ingredient is white sesame seeds: these are not expensive and are available from Japanese, Chinese and Indian grocers.

Finally, note that Japanese sugar is like Western caster sugar (ordinary granulated sugar can be put through a coffee grinder or other food processor for this), and they use coarse sea salt for cooking rather than our refined table salt (any supermarket should stock sea salt). Instant *dashi*, for making fish stock, may be bought in packets in Japanese and some Chinese shops.

Simmering (*nimono*)

Simmering is one of the commonest methods of cooking in Japan. Almost every main meal includes a simmered dish, perhaps not as a main dish, but as one of the accompanying smaller dishes. Simmered dishes basically consist of vegetables, fish or meat, or a combination of these, cooked for varying lengths of time in a seasoned stock. It is of paramount importance that all the different ingredients should finish cooking at the same time, and that none should overcook.

There are no set sizes or shapes for the ingredients, but they must be cut small enough to cook evenly and to be eaten with chopsticks after cooking. Often vegetables, particularly carrots, are cut into flower or other decorative shapes to add to the visual appeal of the finished dish. For this the Japanese use a small cutter, similar in design to Western pastry-cutters. After the whole carrot has been shaped, it is cut into slices of the required thickness. More traditional cooks make flower shapes by scraping the carrot, then cutting five V-shaped indentations down its length before slicing (see illustration opposite).

The skill in cooking a simmered dish lies in developing the flavour of each ingredient and controlling the heat so that it cooks to its best advantage. For many simmered dishes the Japanese use a wooden 'drop lid' (*otoshi-buta*), which sits directly on the meat or vegetables, holding them under the surface of the stock, and encourages them to cook evenly. It also prevents the food from moving about in the currents of liquid and helps the pieces keep their shape. These lids are made of solid rounds of wood, cut about 1 cm (½ inch) smaller in diameter than the inside of the pan (see illustration overleaf). They should always be made wet before use. Japanese grocers in London stock them, but a DIY version can easily be made from an offcut of wood with a handle screwed into the centre of the top. Another possible substitute is a small moulded bamboo plate; these are usually to be found in Chinese arts and crafts shops.

Some of the ingredients in a simmered dish may be par-boiled, and others either shallow- or deep-fried in the preliminary stages, but they are never marinated in advance since all the seasonings for these dishes come from the stock in which the food is finally cooked. Cooking times differ for each recipe and type of food; sometimes a dish is left to marinate in the stock after cooking then served cold, or re-heated just before the meal. For the cook, therefore, a simmered dish has the great advantage of needing no last-minute attention. It can often be made well in advance and put on one side until the rest of the meal is cooked.

Cod slices with ginger

Serves 4

350 g (12 oz) cod fillets or haddock fillets

——

Seasoning stock:
200 ml ($\frac{1}{3}$ pint) water
15 ml (1 tablespoon) *sake*, or 7.5 ml ($1\frac{1}{2}$ teaspoons) vodka and 7.5 ml ($1\frac{1}{2}$ teaspoons) water
30 ml (2 tablespoons) *mirin*, or extra 15 ml (1 tablespoon) caster sugar
30 ml (2 tablespoons) caster sugar
pinch of salt
45 ml (3 tablespoons) soy sauce
12 g ($\frac{1}{2}$ oz) ginger
shreds of lemon peel, very finely cut

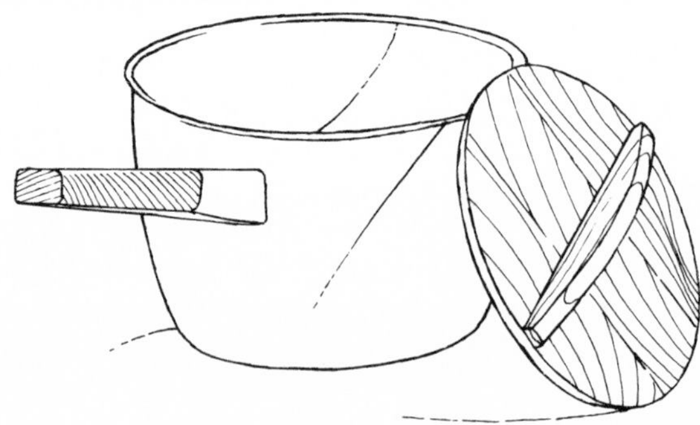

Wash and cut the fish diagonally into slices about 4 cm ($1\frac{1}{2}$ inches) wide. Pat dry. Mix the seasoning sauce in a frying-pan and bring to the boil. Put in the fish slices so they do not overlap and simmer for 15 minutes over a moderate heat covered by a drop lid (see above). From time to time baste the fish with the liquid. Meanwhile grate the ginger and squeeze the juice from the pulp. Discard the dry pulp, and add the ginger juice to the pan. Cook for another minute before serving in four small dishes with a little of the sauce spooned over each helping. Garnish with the shreds of lemon peel.

Braised potatoes with chicken and ginger

Serves 4

This would not be served as a main dish in a Japanese meal, but is typical of the small simmered dishes often served to accompany a main grilled or fried dish.

500 g (1 lb) waxy potatoes
30 ml (2 tablespoons) frozen peas
10 ml (2 teaspoons) finely chopped ginger
150 g (5 oz) minced chicken
30 ml (2 tablespoons) oil
15 ml (1 tablespoon) caster sugar
30 ml (2 tablespoons) *mirin*, or extra 15 ml (1 tablespoon) caster sugar
45 ml (3 tablespoons) soy sauce

Thickening paste:
15 ml (1 tablespoon) cornflour
45 ml (3 tablespoons) water

Peel the potatoes and cut into equal bite-sized pieces. Put the peas into boiling water and boil for 1 minute, then drain. Heat a saucepan with the oil and stir-fry the ginger and chicken for 3 minutes. Add the potatoes, then pour in 750 ml (1¼ pints) water. When the water boils, skim off the scum and turn down the heat. Add the sugar and *mirin*, cover with a drop lid (see opposite) and cook over a moderate heat for 4 minutes. Then add the soy sauce, cover with the drop lid again and simmer until the liquid is reduced by two-thirds (about 20 minutes). Shake the pan several times towards the end of the cooking to coat the potatoes in the sauce. Thicken with the cornflour paste and serve in four individual bowls garnished with the green peas.

Grilling and glazing (*yakimono*)

In direct contrast to simmered dishes, grilled or glazed dishes are cooked very quickly, often after being marinated. They are usually served as a main dish, though small kebabs on skewers are sometimes served as a snack with drinks. Grills of fish or chicken legs are cooked by direct heat, either over charcoal or gas or under an electric grill. Skewers are carefully pushed through the meat or fish so that it holds its shape during cooking, and the food is turned only once.

There are two basic types of grilling in Japanese cooking. One is salt-grilling, used only for fish: the fish is sprinkled with sea salt, then grilled with no further marinade or basting, as in the following recipe.

Salt-grilled mackerel fillets

Serves 4

1 large mackerel
5–10 ml (1–2 teaspoons) coarse sea salt
lemon peel, cut into hairlike threads

Clean and fillet the mackerel, leaving on the skin. Cut each fillet into 7-cm (3-inch) lengths. Skewer each portion of mackerel with two skewers running parallel to each other across the fish from the belly to the back. (This is to hold the pieces of fish flat while cooking.) Sprinkle the salt over the skin of each piece and leave for 20 minutes to marinate. Heat the grill and put the fish, skin-side-up, underneath for 5 minutes. Turn the pieces over and grill the underside for another 5 minutes. Remove the fish from the grill, pull out the skewers carefully so as not to break the fish and arrange the pieces on four heated plates. Garnish with the lemon threads and serve immediately.

For the other type of Japanese grilling a soy sauce and sugar seasoning is used, either as a marinade or as a glaze towards the end of the cooking, or both. The basic sauce for this style of grilling is called *teriyaki* sauce: 45 ml (3 tablespoons) soy sauce, 45 ml (3 tablespoons) *sake*, 45 ml (3 tablespoons) *mirin* and 7.5 ml (1½ teaspoons) caster sugar. Almost all the recipes for grilling with soy sauce and sugar can also be cooked in a frying-pan using a little oil. These are called glazed dishes. The seasoning sauce is added gradually, and the cooking continues until the food is well coated in a shiny glaze and the pan almost dry.

Glazed chicken legs with calabrese

Serves 4

8 small chicken drumsticks
250 g (8 oz) calabrese
15 ml (1 tablespoon) oil

———

Seasoning sauce:
30 ml (2 tablespoons) soy sauce
30 ml (2 tablespoons) *mirin* or
15 ml (1 tablespoon) caster sugar and
7.5 ml (½ tablespoon) water and
7.5 ml (½ tablespoon) vodka
30 ml (2 tablespoons) water
15 ml (1 tablespoon) made English mustard

Bone the drumsticks, keeping the meat in one piece. To do this, cut around the knuckle end of the drumstick to free the ligaments, then slit right up the inside of the leg. Through the incision, carefully cut the bones free from the flesh. Prick the chicken all over with a fork.

Wash and trim the calabrese and cook in boiling salted water until just tender (about 7 minutes, depending on size). Drain well, divide into florets and keep warm.

Heat a frying-pan just big enough to hold the chicken and add the oil. Fry over a high heat until the chicken is browned all over. Then pour away any remaining oil, reduce the heat and, when the pan has cooled, pour in about one-quarter of the seasoning sauce. Continue cooking over a moderate heat for about 8 minutes, turning from time to time and adding more seasoning sauce as the pan dries. Towards the end shake the pan to coat the chicken completely in the sauce. Remove from the heat and cut into bite-sized pieces. Serve on individual plates garnished with the calabrese.

Deep-frying (*agemono*)

Deep-fried foods are one of the great delights of Japanese cuisine. The skill which Japanese cooks display in deep-frying battered foods (*tempura*) is unrivalled. Fish, meat and vegetables are all deep-fried. Vegetables are often cooked without any batter or other coating, but protein foods such as fish, meat and beancurd always have some sort of a film between them and the hot fat. At its simplest this coating can be flour, such as *kudzu* flour, but there are many different batter and coating recipes, including some made of rice noodles or breadcrumbs. Japanese breadcrumbs are similar to coarse home-made breadcrumbs, not in the least like the highly coloured fine-crumb commercial sort sold in the West.

Japanese cooks do not use a basket with deep-fat pans, but prefer to handle the foods with long wooden chopsticks. (It can be a great advantage in all forms of cooking to learn to use such chopsticks in place of tongs, since they are very precise and can be used to pick up both big and very small pieces of food.)

Deep-fried squid

Serves 4

500 g (1 lb) squid
30 ml (2 tablespoons) *sake* or
 15 ml (1 tablespoon) vodka and
 15 ml (1 tablespoon) water
30 ml (2 tablespoons) flour
1 egg, beaten
50 g (2 oz) home-made coarse
 breadcrumbs
oil for deep frying

Clean and skin the squid as directed on page 55. Reserve the fins and tentacles for a salad. Cut the main body into rings about 1 cm (½ inch) wide, and marinate in the *sake* (or vodka and water) for 15 minutes. Dry on a kitchen towel and dust with the flour. Dip into the beaten egg, then coat with the breadcrumbs. Leave to rest for about 3 minutes, then deep-fry at a high heat for 3 minutes. Drain and serve arranged on individual plates. Serve a little worcestershire sauce or plain soy sauce in a small dish as an accompaniment.

An alternative method of cutting the squid is to open out the body sac and score a criss-cross diamond pattern all over the outside (skin side) of the body. Then cut into rectangles about 8 × 3 cm (3 × 1 inches) and marinate as above.

Vegetables and salads

The Japanese housewife has a very wide variety of both green and root vegetables available to her at different times of the year, which she uses to reflect the changing seasons in her meals. She has a number of basic preparation methods. For example, green vegetables are only very lightly boiled in salted water, then immediately plunged into cold water to stop any further cooking and to help them keep their bright colour; after this they are either well drained or squeezed dry before being seasoned. Cucumbers are rolled vigorously on a board strewn with salt to draw out the water in them, then rinsed well.

The simplest seasoning for green vegetables is a light sprinkling of soy sauce, but vinegar dressings are frequently used with lightly cooked or raw vegetables. Two-flavoured vinegar for dressing a salad is made with 25 ml (1½ tablespoons) rice vinegar and 5 ml (1 teaspoon) salt. Another version can be made with 25 ml (1½ tablespoons) rice vinegar and 10 ml (2 teaspoons) soy sauce. Three-flavoured vinegar is made with 25 ml (1½ tablespoons) rice vinegar (or 15 ml/1 tablespoon cider vinegar and 10 ml/2 teaspoons water), 10 ml (2 teaspoons) soy sauce and 5 ml (1 teaspoon) caster sugar.

French bean salad

Serves 4

180 g (6 oz) french beans

Dressing:
25 ml (1½ tablespoons) soy sauce
10 ml (2 teaspoons) *sake* or 5 ml (1 teaspoon) vodka and 5 ml (1 teaspoon) water
5 ml (1 teaspoon) *mirin* or 2.5 ml (½ teaspoon) sugar and 2.5 ml (½ teaspoon) water
7 g (¼ oz) ginger

2.5 ml (½ teaspoon) white sesame seeds

Top and tail the beans, and string if necessary. Boil in lightly salted water for 5 minutes, then rinse in cold water and drain well. Mix the dressing. Grate the ginger and squeeze out the ginger juice from the pulp into the dressing. Discard the dry pulp. Toast the sesame seeds in a dry pan over a moderate heat until golden brown. Shake or stir continually to prevent burning. Then leave to cool. Toss the beans in the dressing and divide between four small plates. Sprinkle with toasted sesame seeds before serving.

Broccoli with a mustard dressing

Serves 4

This simple broccoli salad has a vinegar dressing made more interesting by the inclusion of a little mustard. It could also be made with french beans or okra.

250 g (8 oz); broccoli (calabrese or purple sprouting)

Dressing:
30 ml (2 tablespoons) rice vinegar or 15 ml (1 tablespoon) cider vinegar and 15 ml (1 tablespoon) water
10 ml (2 teaspoons) caster sugar
15 ml (1 tablespoon) soy sauce
2.5 ml (½ teaspoon) made English mustard

Trim and cut the broccoli into small florets. If using calabrese, pare the skin from the thick central stalk and discard, and cut the stalk into batons about 5 cm (2 inches) long and 1 cm (½ inch) square. Boil the broccoli or calabrese in lightly salted water for 4 minutes. Then immediately plunge into cold water. Drain well. Just before serving mix the dressing and sprinkle it over the broccoli. Serve in small individual dishes.

Clear soups

Japanese clear soups are always made either with chicken stock, as in the recipe below, or with *dashi*, a stock made from seaweed and dried fish flakes (see page 130). These stocks can be seasoned to taste with soy sauce, salt or *sake*, then garnished with a range of vegetables such as carrots, white radish, spinach, watercress, french beans, Chinese leaves, leeks or cucumber, and seafood, fish or chicken. The vegetables, fish and chicken can be cut into any size of shreds, slices or pieces suitable for eating with chopsticks. Root vegetables are par-boiled until almost soft, other green vegetables blanched then refreshed in cold water. Raw cucumber, watercress and very finely sliced leeks may be placed in soup bowls and have the boiling stock poured over them. Seafood, fish and chicken are all cooked either in the stock or separately, then united in the soup just before serving. The Japanese do not use spoons for eating soup, but eat the solids with chopsticks and drink the soup.

Clear soup with chicken and vegetables

Serves 4

1 chicken thigh
15 ml (1 tablespoon) *sake* or
 7.5 ml (1½ teaspoons) vodka and
 7.5 ml (1½ teaspoons) water
2.5 ml (½ teaspoon) salt
1 litre (1¾ pints) chicken stock
50 g (2 oz) carrot
50 g (2 oz) young leek (white
 only)

Marinate the chicken in the *sake* and salt for 20 minutes. Then put into the chicken stock and simmer gently for 30 minutes. Skim off any scum that rises to the surface. Remove the chicken from the stock and when cool enough to handle take out the bone. Cut the meat into bite-sized pieces. Leave the stock to cool, then skim off any fat. Cut the carrot into thin oblongs 1 × 4 cm (¼ × 1½ inches). Par-boil in salted water until just soft. Then drain and reserve. Wash and trim the leek and cut into very thin slices. Shake to free the rings. Re-heat the stock and adjust the seasoning with salt if necessary. Return the chicken to the stock for 2 minutes to warm through. Arrange the slices of carrot and leek rings in the pre-heated soup bowls, divide the chicken pieces between them and ladle over the boiling stock. Serve at once.

Garnishes

Part of the attraction of Japanese food is the variety and colour given to dishes by different garnishes and seasonings. Almost every dish will have some form of additional garnish, no matter how it has been cooked. One of the most common is the grated pulp of white radish. As a variant, 3 dried chillis can be pushed into holes made with a chopstick in a 5-cm (2-inch) length of white radish, then the two grated together. Both the plain and the chillied white radish pulp should be squeezed dry before being shaped into tiny mounds on the serving dishes.

Fresh ginger may be grated and used in the same fashion, or shredded extremely finely, then sprinkled over the dish, or piled beside it. Pickled red ginger (either home-made, see page 158, or bought), cut into thin strips, brings both colour and flavour to a dish.

Other garnishes include finely chopped spring onions, thin shreds of toasted *nori* seaweed, or the zest of a *yuzu* (a Japanese citrus fruit, for which lemon or bitter orange may be substituted), cut into threads or into small oblongs slashed and bent into triangles. Dried fish flakes (*hanakatsuo*), poppy seeds, sesame seeds, *wasabi* mustard, seven-spice pepper and dried chilli flakes are all used as additional seasonings for different dishes, while grilled green peppers, lengths of leek or deep-fried slices of sweet potato are used to vary colour and texture.

Serving a Japanese meal

A great deal more importance is attached to the serving of even a simple meal at home in Japan than is normal in the West. The final visual effect of a dish is given as much care and thought as its initial preparation and cooking. Japanese tableware is very varied. There is no such thing as a dinner service: each set of dishes or bowls used is individually chosen to suit a particular dish. A Japanese household has numerous sets of small dishes, both round and square, oblong plates and small shallow bowls of different colours, textures and designs, rather as in the West we have various containers for flower arrangements. Serving a meal is like painting a picture with food, and as satisfying. Rather romantically, many Japanese claim that the inspirations for their food arrangements come from the natural scenery of their country, with its mountains, lakes, forests and plains.

There are a few basic rules for the arrangement of foods. A grilled fish laid on a flat dish should face the left and lie at a slight angle with its tail further away from the diner than its head. A fillet of fish is always placed with the skin away from the diner. Simmered foods should be arranged in dishes so that the largest and most important item is at the back of the bowl, away from the diner, with the second most important in front to the left and the third or smallest to the right. Any big piece of food on a plate will generally have some garnish to go with it. This can either be sprinkled over it or laid to one side at the front of the dish. Salads and other foods should, if possible, not touch the sides of the bowl but be piled in mounds in the middle.

Just as there are rules for the planning and presentation of dishes, so there are rules for the laying out of a meal (see illustration on opposite page).

Planning a Japanese meal

There is a clear distinction in Japan between a formal meal, usually for a special occasion or for visitors, and the main family meal of the day. The family meal is eaten between 6 and 7 pm, but often the husband/father of the family will come in later and eat by himself. In a family meal all the dishes are served at once, but every diner has his own separate helping of each dish served on individual plates and bowls. Traditionally each diner would also have his own small table. There is no allowance for second helpings in a Japanese meal, except for the rice, of which it is customary to eat several bowlfuls.

Japanese menus are based on odd numbers of dishes, in addition to the soup and rice. Often, although not traditional, a meal will end with raw fruit such as melon, peaches or grapes in the summer, oranges or tangerines in the winter; the traditional end to the meal is a tiny cup of green tea. The Japanese never have puddings or desserts as is normal in the West. Such desserts or sweets as they have are eaten in mid-afternoon in place of afternoon tea.

A typical family meal of three dishes will have one big dish (Chapter 4) and one small dish (Chapter 5), each cooked by a different method. The third dish will be a small salad (Chapter 6). These will all be served together with a soup (probably made with *miso*), pickles and rice. The menu for such a meal might be salt-grilled fish, simmered white radish with a *miso* dressing, and chicken and *wakame* salad together with a *miso* and beancurd soup, rice and pickles.

When a Japanese housewife plans a meal she chooses the ingredients with the season very much in mind. She strives to add interest by creating contrasts of colour and flavour between the different dishes. A typical family meal chosen from the recipes in this chapter might consist of deep-fried squid, braised potatoes with chicken and ginger, broccoli with a mustard dressing, and clear soup with chicken and vegetables, served with plain boiled rice and tea.

A more elaborate family meal of five dishes – possibly for a special occasion – might include *sashimi* and another big dish; or if no *sashimi* two big dishes, each cooked in a different style, and two small dishes,

also produced by different cooking methods, and a salad with perhaps several ingredients and an elaborate dressing. The dishes chosen for such a meal might be *sashimi* of fresh salmon, grilled chicken legs with poppy seeds, simmered sweet potatoes with mixed vegetables, 'a thousand grasses' (steamed savoury custard) and ham salad, together with a clear soup with slices of sea bass, rice and pickles. An alternative scheme might include two elaborate salads and only one small dish.

It is not easy to serve a big Japanese meal with successive dishes and still sit down with one's visitors, but equally if there are several dishes it is not really satisfactory to produce them all at once. Therefore for this book a system has been devised (which is *not* Japanese) of breaking the meal into sections or courses. A meal with five dishes can be divided into a grilled dish with a salad, followed by a simmered dish together with a fried dish, and another salad or a steamed dish, and finally, as the last course, soup, rice and pickles. After this fresh fruit can be served as a dessert. Seven or nine dishes can be grouped into four courses following the same system, which allows the hostess to sit with her guests and still do the cooking.

Formal meals, almost invariably restaurant meals in Japan, have seven or nine dishes, and a different, stricter form of planning and service is usual. The dishes are served in sequence, starting with an *hors d'oeuvre*, then a clear soup followed by *sashimi* and then a grilled dish. These would be followed by a big simmered dish, after which would come a small dish, either steamed or deep-fried, then a salad. The meal would end with a *miso* soup, pickles and rice. For a nine-dish meal, both a steamed and deep-fried dish would be served as well as two styles of salad. It can be seen from this that in Japanese meals, and formal ones in particular, considerable attention is paid to the manner of cooking used for each dish; certain styles of cooking such as grilling and simmering take precedence over others such as steaming and deep-frying.

It may be some comfort for the harassed cook to know that it is normal practice in Japan to cook some dishes well in advance of the meal, and that there is no general expectation in Japanese cuisine that all dishes will be served piping hot straight from the oven or pan. In the winter, however, some dishes are re-heated just before being served. A Japanese meal will always include some cold dishes. Generally speaking, a meal would seem incomplete to the Japanese unless it included some fish in at least one dish. The everyday soup is *miso* soup and there are an infinite number of garnishes to go with it, ranging from cockles to beancurd. However, *miso* soup is never served as the main soup at a formal meal.

What to drink with a Japanese meal

Sake, a fortified rice wine, is the normal drink for formal meals in Japan, as well as at other times. It should be warmed to blood heat before it is served. It may be drunk throughout the meal until the final *miso* soup and rice are served, but once the rice has appeared all drinking is traditionally supposed to stop. The Japanese also drink spirits such as whisky with a meal, or their own light wines made from Japanese grapes. If you wish to drink wine with a Japanese meal in the West, a dry German white wine or a Muscat d'Alsace would be suitable.

The Japanese brew a beer rather like Western bitter which they also drink with meals.

For more humble meals the coarsest grade of green tea – *bancha* – is a very good thirst-quencher, drunk towards the end of the meal. It goes particularly well with rice. To make green tea, use almost-boiling water and leave to infuse for 1–2 minutes in the teapot. Then pour out the tea, draining all the liquid from the tea leaves. If Japanese green tea leaves are left to infuse any longer the tea will lose its delicate flavour and become bitter. The pot can be re-filled with fresh hot water when another cup is required.

As an alternative a more delicate green tea – *sencha* – may be served after a meal, in tiny, bowl-shaped cups. This is also made with not-quite-boiling water, but should infuse for only 1 minute before being completely drained off.

Japanese dishes in Western meals

In contrast to the generally rather unhappy result of including dishes from cuisines of different cultures in one Western-style meal, many

Japanese dishes blend well with Western ones. Among those which are particularly suitable are salt-grilled or *miso*-grilled fish, various grilled chicken dishes, and deep-fried fish and seafood coated in Japanese *tempura* batters. Many Japanese salads make interesting and unusual side salads in a Western meal. A clear *dashi* soup with cubes of silk beancurd makes a pleasing variation on *consommé royale*, and involves much less work. However, experience suggests that simmered and steamed dishes are less satisfactory when combined with Western dishes.

Since many Japanese recipes are devised on the assumption that the whole meal will comprise several dishes, remember to increase the quantities when using a Japanese recipe for a main dish in a Western meal. There is of course no need in this case to serve the food on individual plates.

Main dishes

In Japan, as in other countries, the main dishes of a meal are those that are biggest, cost the most and are most carefully prepared. Unless the meal is specifically vegetarian the main dish will be made with fish, or meat, or occasionally beancurd, and will include vegetables only as a garnish. Any cooking method may be used but in any one meal the methods used for each dish must be different. Some cooking – or non-cooking – styles are reserved for main dishes: for example, *sashimi* (raw fish) and grills are always main dishes, while simmering or deep-frying may be used for main or for secondary dishes.

Fish

The range of fresh fish regularly available in Japan is much greater than in the UK. However, as the choice of wet fish is said to be improving recipes have been included for some fish that are not necessarily available in all markets for those who may be lucky enough to find them on sale. The Japanese consider the freshness of fish to be of paramount importance. Currently shoppers are complaining in Tokyo and other large towns that fresh fish is no longer so readily available; none the less, every local shopping centre in the big towns and large country villages has at least one fresh-fish shop, as was common in the UK thirty or forty years ago. Some frozen fish is sold in the large supermarkets, but noticeably more people, even in the supermarkets, are to be seen choosing fish from the long fresh-fish counters than at the smaller frozen-fish cabinets. On the whole the Japanese judge 'freshness' by length of time dead rather than lack of decay, as is customary in freezer-dominated markets.

Obviously fish that are common in Japanese waters will not always be the same as those regularly caught in the Atlantic Ocean and North Sea, so the cooking of Japanese fish dishes in the UK will often be an exercise in compromise and adaptation. See page 166 for a list of fresh fish occasionally available in UK markets and suitable for various Japanese dishes.

Preparation of fish

Just as the actual types of fish eaten in Japan are different from those in the UK so are some of the methods of preparation.

Any fish with scales that is not to have its skin removed should first be de-scaled. Do this by running a blunt knife from tail to head on both sides of the body to lift off the scales. The loose scales are easier to control if this is done under running water. The filleting of any fish is basically the same as in the West, as is the gutting of a flat fish to be cooked whole, but whole round fish, particularly if they are to be grilled, are gutted differently: lay the fish with its head facing the right and its stomach towards you; with one hand holding the fish's head, slide a sharp, pointed knife through the gill opening and cut the thin membrane dividing the gills from the stomach cavity; then, with the back of the point of the knife, hook out the stomach and gently pull free all the viscera; when the stomach cavity is empty, cut out all the gills from both sides of the head through the same gill opening (see illustration below); rinse very thoroughly, running water right through the fish. It is most important that the fish is completely gutted and well cleaned with running water. If necessary slide a finger into the bigger fish, such as mackerel, to make sure the fish is quite clean.

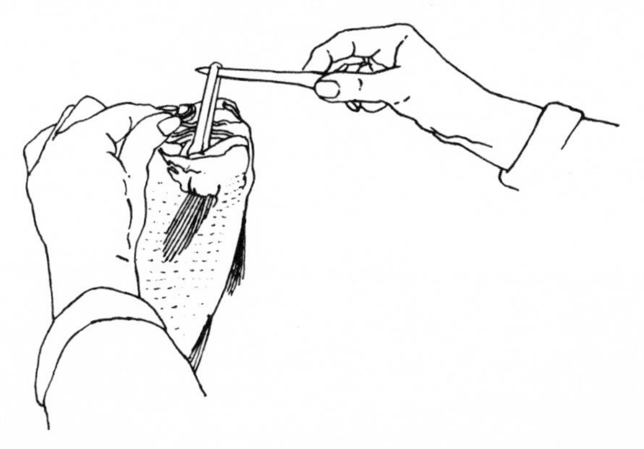

If a fish has been gutted in this manner it will look totally untouched when served facing to the left of the diner, whereas a fish whose stomach has been split open will twist and distort during the cooking. This method of gutting fish is very easy with fresh fish, but not so easy with stale or frozen fish, since both gut and flesh are apt to tear.

Japanese cooks usually push two skewers through each fish before grilling, so that it keeps its shape. This is easy and very satisfactory, but not essential. To do it lay the fish facing to the right and pass one skewer in above the eye, to come out about one-third down the length of the body. Go in again after another third and come out finally at the top of the tail.

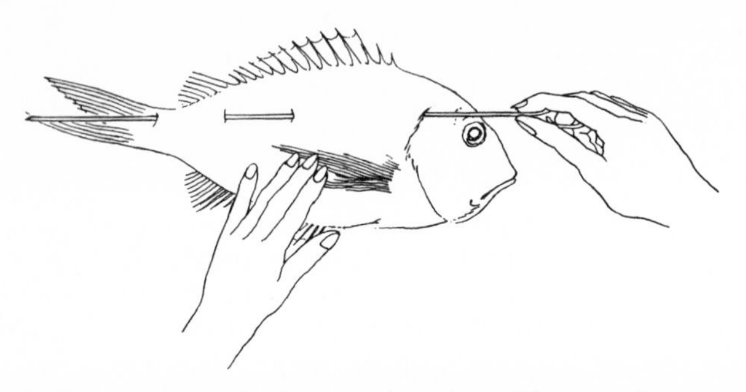

The second skewer goes in just under the gill, out about one-third down the body, in again and out at the base of the tail.

The skewers should cross beyond the fish's tail.

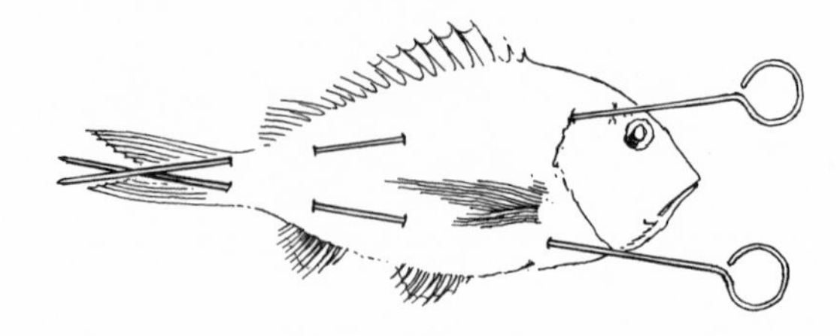

It is most important that the skewers at no time show on the left-hand side of the fish, and that this side remains unmarked to be presented

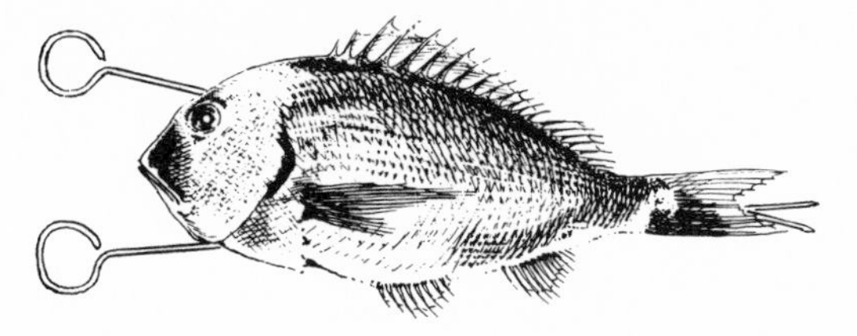

uppermost, facing left, when the fish is served. Fillets of fish are skewered to hold them spread out and flat, usually using two skewers to each fillet.

Sashimi (raw fish)

Raw fish has pride of place in a Japanese meal. Contrary to some Westerners' nervous expectations, there is no fishiness about its taste whatsoever, but a fresh and most delicate flavour. Tremendous care and thought goes into its presentation – including the choice of plates on which it is to be served. Often *sashimi* is extremely expensive since only the very best cuts of the freshest fish are used. Although *sashimi* is always part of an important meal, it is not normally prepared at home. For special occasions it is ordered (ready sliced and beautifully arranged) from the local fishmonger. However, it is not in itself hard to make, provided the proper ingredients are at hand. Do not try to make *sashimi* unless you are certain that the fish is really fresh, or even better have seen it caught or caught it yourself. Tired or stale fish will be a disaster. Restaurants in Japan often keep fish for *sashimi* alive in tanks until they are required, to ensure absolute freshness. In the UK really fresh salmon trout are to be found in good fishmongers during the season April to July, while fresh rainbow trout are sold all the year round in the various fish farms to be found near most big towns. Fresh tunny, sea bass and squid all make good *sashimi*, but it is a mistake to attempt it using frozen fish.

Fish for *sashimi* can be cleaned and filleted in the normal Western manner in advance of the meal provided it is kept cold in the meantime; but the final skinning and slicing should be done only minutes before it is served. To skin a fish fillet, lay the fillet skin-side-down on a flat surface. Starting from the tail end hold the skin down while lifting off the flesh with a sharp knife held at an angle of 45 degrees to the fish. Always work towards the head. To get a firm grip on the skin dip your thumb and forefinger in a little salt.

There are two basic methods of cutting fish for *sashimi*: wafer-thin slices cut across the grain, or chunky slices and strips cut with the

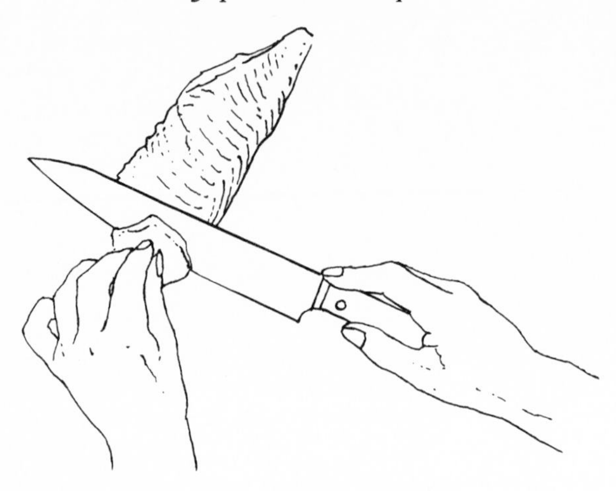

grain. For the former, lay the skinned fillet skin-side-up and slice across the grain of the fish at an angle of about 45 degrees (see above diagram). Lay the transparently thin slices straight on a big plate in the form of a circle.

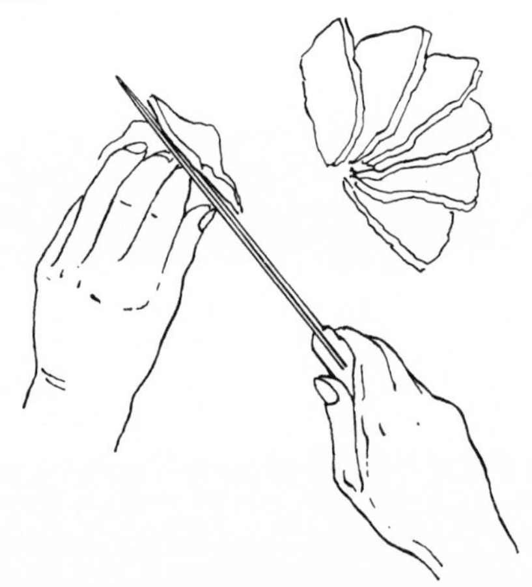

The other way of cutting *sashimi* is to start with the fillet skin-side-up but with the knife held at a right angle to it, and cut $\frac{1}{2}$ cm ($\frac{1}{4}$ inch)-thick slices straight down through the fish (see above).

Various accompaniments can be served with *sashimi*, but none is essential. Sometimes it is served with very finely shredded white radish, or cucumber, or the fish slices may be laid on an ice cube, in which case a grille is put underneath so that the ice water may drain away. Often *sashimi* is served only with seasonings such as grated ginger, squeezed dry in a clean cloth and put into a small rounded heap on the plate, or a similar mound of grated white radish and dried chillis (see page 37) or a cone of *wasabi* mustard. Colour and interest can be added with a leaf or two of watercress or a frond of green fennel.

There are several dipping sauces that go with *sashimi*, depending on the taste of the diner, or the type of fish. The simplest is soy sauce and *sake* in 3 to 1 proportions, to which the diners add *wasabi* or grated ginger to taste. Another dipping sauce is made with 45 ml (3 tablespoons) soy sauce, 15 ml (1 tablespoon) *sake* and 15 ml (1 tablespoon) *hanakatsuo*. Bring to the boil and simmer for 3 minutes, then allow to cool before straining and serving in individual small bowls. Yet another dipping sauce that can be served with *sashimi* is the lemony *ponzu* sauce described on page 72.

Grilled and glazed fish

Salt-grilled sea bream

Serves 4

The Japanese have a variety of red sea bream (*Chrysophrys major*) which they call '*tai*', a pun on the word for luck. There are many 'lucky' foods and food puns such as this in both Japanese and Chinese cuisine. Because of the underlying idea of good fortune for the diner, '*tai*' are always served at weddings in Japan. Unfortunately this particular variety of sea bream, which is especially good to eat, does not live in British waters, and we must make do with a rather less delicate fish of the same family (*Pagrus pagrus*).

4 small sea bream
10 ml (2 teaspoons) coarse sea salt

Scale the fish by running a blunt knife along the sides of the fish from the tail to the head against the lie of the scales. It makes less mess if this is done under running water. Leaving on the heads, clean and skewer the fish as described on pages 43–5. Take a spine from one lower fin and insert across the base of the front spine of the dorsal fin: this will hold the fin erect during the cooking.

Sprinkle each fish with salt, especially the fins and tail, and lay them over a moderate to low heat. (Two bricks covered in tinfoil can be stood on either side of an ordinary gas ring to make a primitive indoor barbeque.) Put the left side of the fish, which has no skewers, towards the heat first. Turn only once during the cooking, which takes about 15 minutes. Make sure the heat is low enough to allow the fish to cook right through before the skin becomes too brown.

Alternatively, omit the skewering but pin the dorsal fin and salt the fish as above, then lay them, facing left, on an ordinary grill rack under a Western-type grill. Turn after about 5 minutes and continue grilling until cooked. Serve immediately the fish is cooked.

Trout or fresh red mullet can be grilled whole in the same manner.

Salt-grilled sea bass fillets

Serves 4

750 g ($1\frac{1}{2}$ lb) sea bass
5–10 ml (1–2 teaspoons) coarse sea salt
red pickled ginger

Fillet the sea bass but leave on the skin. Cut each fillet into 7-cm (3-inch) lengths, and skewer each piece of fish with two skewers running parallel to each other across the fish from the thickest part to the thinnest. Sprinkle the salt over the skin of each piece and leave for 10 minutes to marinate. Meanwhile heat the grill to moderately hot. Put the fish, skin-side-up, under the grill for 5 minutes, then turn the pieces over and grill the underside for another 5 minutes. Remove the skewers and arrange the pieces of fish on four individual flat plates. Garnish with a little pile of red ginger strips and serve immediately.

Grilled trout with miso

Serves 4

4 small trout
60 ml (4 tablespoons) light *miso*
25 ml ($1\frac{1}{2}$ tablespoons) *sake*

Wash the fish and, leaving the heads on, clean as directed on page 43. Rinse the stomach cavities very thoroughly with running water. Pat the fish dry and roll each trout in a clean piece of cheesecloth. Mix the *miso* and *sake* into a soft paste and smear this over the cheesecloth on both sides of each trout. Make sure they are all well coated in the paste, then leave to marinate for 6–12 hours, depending on the weather.

Strip off the cloth and wipe away any remaining *miso* from the fish. Grill on a rack under a high heat for about 5 minutes per side. Serve hot on individual plates.

Small mackerel can be marinated in the same way before grilling.

Grilled salmon steaks with a sweet soy sauce

Serves 4

Traditional Japanese cooks use skewers to hold these steaks while they are grilled over the heat, rather than under it. Skewers have been omitted in this recipe since it has been adapted to suit a Western-type grill.

2 fresh salmon steaks, about 125 g (4 oz) each

Marinade:
10 ml (2 teaspoons) caster sugar
25 ml (1½ tablespoons) *mirin*
45 ml (3 tablespoons) soy sauce

shredded toasted *nori* and pickled ginger shreds to garnish

Remove the centre bones from the steaks and divide each in half. Marinate for 2 hours, turning from time to time in the marinade. Pre-heat the grill and put the steaks under it at a moderate heat. Baste with the remaining marinade during the cooking. After about 6 minutes turn and cook the steaks on the other side, basting as before until cooked. Serve on four individual plates garnished with shreds of toasted *nori* and with a tiny pile of pickled ginger at the side.

Grilled mackerel with ginger

Serves 4

1 large mackerel

Marinade:
30 ml (2 tablespoons) *mirin*
15 ml (1 tablespoon) *sake*
45 ml (3 tablespoons) soy sauce
15 g (½ oz) ginger, cut into very fine threads
1 clove garlic, crushed (optional)*

Cut off the head and clean the mackerel. Wash well and cut into steaks about 4 cm (1½ inches) thick. Marinate for 1 hour. Heat the grill. Grill the steaks under a moderate heat for about 5 minutes, brushing once with the remaining marinade. Turn over and continue cooking and basting for a further 5–7 minutes. Serve hot on individual plates.

Glazed cod steaks

Serves 4

It seems likely that this form of grilling (*teriyaki*) using oil came from the French style of shallow-frying fish, and is a relatively recent adoption. Traditionally the word *teriyaki* implies the use of skewers rather than frying in oil.

2 cod steaks, about 175 g (6 oz) each

Marinade:
10 ml (2 teaspoons) caster sugar
25 ml (1½ tablespoons) *mirin*
45 ml (3 tablespoons) soy sauce

flour for dusting
15 ml (1 tablespoon) oil

* Garlic is not particularly Japanese, but does improve the dish.

Choose steaks about 1½ cm (½ inch) thick. Cut each in half and remove the bones. Marinate for about 8 minutes. Then pat the steaks dry with kitchen paper and lightly dust with flour. Reserve the marinade. Heat a frying-pan with the oil, and fry the steaks over a moderate heat until almost cooked, turning once. Remove any remaining oil from the pan and pour in the marinade. Cover the pan and continue cooking over a moderate heat until the sauce is thick, turning the steaks once. At the end of cooking the steaks should be well coated in the sauce. Lift out and serve on individual plates. Serve either hot or cold.

Glazed sardines with ginger

Serves 4

12 sardines (frozen)

Marinade:
40 ml (2½ tablespoons) soy sauce
10 ml (2 teaspoons) grated ginger

---

flour for dusting
30 ml (2 tablespoons) oil
50 g (2 oz) grated white radish, squeezed dry in a clean cloth

Scale the thawed sardines, scraping gently from tail to head under running water. Then gut as directed on page 43, keeping whole. Marinate for 40 minutes, turning several times in the marinade to coat well. Then drain and dust very lightly with flour. Heat the oil in a large frying-pan. Put in the sardines, left sides down. Fry for about 2 minutes, shaking the pan from time to time to prevent sticking. When golden brown underneath turn over and fry on the other side. If necessary turn down the heat until the fish are cooked. Finally turn up the heat again for the final moments of cooking and serve hot. Arrange, three to each plate, all facing left. Garnish with small domes of grated white radish.

Glazed squid

Serves 4

2 small squid, about 250 g (8 oz) each

Seasoning sauce:
30 ml (2 tablespoons) caster sugar
15 ml (1 tablespoon) *mirin*
45 ml (3 tablespoons) soy sauce

---

15 ml (1 tablespoon) oil

Clean and skin the squid as directed on page 55, reserving the tentacles for a salad. Open out the main bodies of the squid and score all over on the skin side with fine criss-cross cuts. Then cut into rectangles about

5 cm (2 inches) long and 2 cm (¾ inch) wide. Have ready the seasoning sauce just at boiling point in a moderate-sized saucepan. Heat a frying-pan with the oil and stir-fry the squid over a very high heat for about 1 minute. Then immediately drop the pieces into the seasoning sauce and, shaking the pan all the time, boil vigorously over a high heat until the rolls of squid are coated in the sauce. Do this very quickly (overcooked squid becomes tough and leathery). Serve hot divided between four small dishes.

Baked mackerel with lemon

Serves 4

250 g (8 oz) fillet of mackerel

Marinade:
15 ml (1 tablespoon) soy sauce
15 ml (1 tablespoon) *mirin*
2.5 ml (½ teaspoon) toasted sesame seeds, lightly crushed

5 g (¼ oz) ginger, finely sliced
1 small slice of fresh fennel bulb, shredded
25 g (1 oz) leek, finely sliced
4 slices of lemon

Dipping sauce:
25 ml (1½ tablespoons) rice vinegar
25 ml (1½ tablespoons) soy sauce
25 ml (1½ tablespoons) *dashi*

Cut the mackerel with the skin side up, holding the knife at an angle of 45 degrees, into thin, slanting slices about 1 cm (½ inch) thick. Marinate for 30 minutes. Cut four 20-cm (8-inch) squares of tinfoil and crinkle slightly. Arrange some mackerel slices in the centre of each and divide the ginger, fennel and leek between them. Turn up the sides to form cups, but do not close. Stand the tinfoil packets in a dry frying-pan and cover with a tight-fitting lid. Cook over a moderate heat for 5 minutes, then add a slice of lemon to the top of each mound of mackerel. Continue cooking as before until the mackerel is cooked (about 6 minutes). Meanwhile mix the dipping sauce and pour into four small dishes. Serve the mackerel emptied from the packets on to individual plates with the lemon slices on top and the small dishes of dipping sauce at the side.

Alternatively, after filling the tinfoil packets, close them up completely and place on an oven tray in a pre-heated oven (180°C, 350°F, Gas 4). Bake for 7 minutes. Then open the packets and slip a slice of lemon on to each. Re-fasten the tinfoil and return to the oven for a further 7 minutes. Serve as above.

Another version of this dish can be made with salmon or cod steaks.

250 g (8 oz) fish steaks (cod or salmon)
30 ml (2 tablespoons) *sake*
pinch of salt
20 g ($\frac{3}{4}$ oz) mixed vegetables, e.g. white of leek, mushroom, carrot, green pepper, finely sliced
4 slices of lemon

Divide the fish steaks into four and remove the bones. Put a portion on each square of oiled tinfoil. Sprinkle with the *sake*, a little salt and the finely sliced mixed vegetables. Lay a lemon slice on top of each, and close the tinfoil tightly. Bake in the oven for 20 minutes, then serve, lifted out of the packets, on individual plates.

Simmered dishes

Simmered dishes from Tokyo and the east of Japan have a fuller flavour, are made with a darker soy sauce and are served with less sauce than those from Kyoto and the west, which are made with a light soy sauce, have a thinner flavour and are served with more sauce.

Simmered herrings in a chilli sauce

1 small leek
4 small herrings, about 180 g (6 oz) each

Seasoning sauce:
45 ml (3 tablespoons) *miso*
15 ml (1 tablespoon) caster sugar
15 ml (1 tablespoon) *mirin*
15 ml (1 tablespoon) *sake*
15 ml (1 tablespoon) soy sauce
120 ml (8 tablespoons) water

---

10 g ($\frac{1}{2}$ oz) ginger, cut into thin slices
1 chilli, either dried or fresh, or more to taste

Wash and trim the leek and cut into 3-cm (1-inch) lengths. Thread on a skewer and grill over a gas or electric ring until slightly browned, then leave on one side.

Scale and gut the herrings according to the directions on page 46, leaving on their heads. Lay flat on the bottom of a large frying-pan, all facing left. Pour over three-quarters of the seasoning sauce and add the ginger and chilli. Bring to the boil over a high heat, then turn down to a moderate heat and simmer for 10 minutes. Pour in the remaining seasoning sauce and baste the fish carefully. Add the leeks and simmer for another 3 minutes, taking care the pan does not become too dry and the fish burn. Serve each fish facing left on a separate plate, with a few slices of leek as garnish.

Simmered mackerel

Serves 4

250 g (8 oz) mackerel fillet
200 g (6 oz) white radish, grated
flour for dusting
oil for deep frying

———

Seasoning sauce:
15 ml (1 tablespoon) *mirin*
15 ml (1 tablespoon) soy sauce
100 ml (3½ fl oz) *dashi*

———

4–5 spring onions, finely chopped
12 slices of deep-fried sweet potato (optional garnish)

Cut the mackerel into bite-sized slices diagonally, with the knife held obliquely to the fish. Grate the white radish, then squeeze the pulp dry in a clean cloth. Dry the mackerel slices on kitchen paper and lightly dust with flour. Heat the deep fat to 170°C (350°F), then drop in the fish slices. Fry for 3 minutes, then lift out and drain. Bring the seasoning sauce to the boil in a saucepan and add the fish slices, the white radish and the spring onions. Continue cooking for another 30 seconds, then lift from the heat.

Serve the mackerel in four small dishes with a little of the seasoning sauce spooned over it. Garnish each plate with the slices of sweet potato. This dish can be served either hot or cold.

To deep-fry sweet potato, peel the potato thickly, then slice into 1-cm (½-inch) slices. Soak in cold water for about 15 minutes to draw out the starch, then drain and pat dry before deep-frying for about 3–4 minutes.

Simmered dabs

Serves 4

4 small dabs

———

Seasoning stock:
200 ml (⅓ pint) water
15 ml (1 tablespoon) *sake*
30 ml (2 tablespoons) caster sugar
30 ml (2 tablespoons) *mirin*
45 ml (3 tablespoons) soy sauce
5 ml (1 teaspoon) grated ginger

———

100 g (4 oz) leek
15 ml (1 tablespoon) soy sauce

Clean the dabs in the normal way. Score the top side of each fish (the brown side) 2–3 times. Mix the seasoning sauce in a large frying-pan and bring to the boil. Put the dabs, brown-side-up, into the pan and bring back to the boil. Spoon the stock over the dabs, and if necessary skim to remove any foam; then cover with a drop lid. Cook at a moderate heat for about 10 minutes until the stock is reduced by a half, occasionally spooning a little cooking liquor over the top of the dabs.

Meanwhile wash and cut the leek into 3-cm (1-inch) lengths. Thread these on a skewer and lightly brown over a gas or electric ring. When the dabs are cooked, add the leek and the additional soy sauce and bring back to the boil. Serve hot on individual plates with the leeks and a little of the cooking liquor spooned over.

Simmered cod steaks with aubergines

Serves 4

300 g (10 oz) cod steak, fresh or frozen
15 ml (1 tablespoon) *sake*
75 g (3 oz) green peppers
100 g (4 oz) aubergine

——

Seasoning sauce:
200 ml ($\frac{1}{3}$ pint) *dashi*
45 ml (3 tablespoons) *mirin*
25 ml ($1\frac{1}{2}$ tablespoons) soy sauce
1 dried chilli (more for a hotter dish)

——

flour for dusting
oil for deep frying

Cut the cod in half and remove the bones. Then cut diagonally into four equal-sized pieces using a knife held at an oblique angle to the fish. Marinate with the *sake* for 20 minutes. Meanwhile de-seed the pepper and cut it into oblong bite-sized pieces. Cut the aubergine into small wedges, each approximately the same size, and slash the skin to half the depth of each wedge with numerous cuts about 2 mm ($\frac{1}{10}$ inch) apart. Soak the wedges in cold water for 10 minutes to remove any bitterness. Mix the seasoning sauce. Heat the oil to 170°C (350°F). Pat the fish dry with kitchen paper and lightly dust with flour. Deep-fry for about 8 minutes, then lift out and drain well. Skim the oil. Dry the aubergines and peppers and deep-fry for 3–5 minutes. Leave to drain while heating the seasoning sauce in a large saucepan. Put in the fish, peppers and aubergine and bring to the boil. Boil for 1 minute, then serve on individual flat dishes with a little of the seasoning sauce spooned over.

Alternatively, the deep frying can if necessary be done well in advance of the meal and the fish and vegetables left to drain until just before they are required, when they can be re-heated in the seasoning sauce and served as above.

Any left-over seasoning sauce from this recipe can be used to cook *okara* (the residue of soya beans left when making beancurd, see page 100).

Stuffed squid

Serves 4

This dish is best made with tiny squid about 13 cm (5 inches) long. However, if these cannot be found use squid weighing not more than 250 g (8 oz) each.

To clean a squid, gently pull the head, tentacles and attached entrails free from the body sac. Cut through the head of the squid just above the eye to remove the tentacles, and reserve. Discard the rest of the head and entrails. Squeeze out the polyp from the centre of the tentacles and discard. Remove the 'bone' from its pocket in the body and discard. Tear off the bottom flaps from the outside of the body and reserve. Rinse out the body sac and peel off the dark skin from the outside.

500 g (1 lb) squid (4 small or 2 large)
1 dried mushroom
100 g (4 oz) beancurd
40 g (1½ oz) carrot
10 snow peas

Seasoning stock for the vegetables:
100 ml (3½ fl oz) *dashi*
15 ml (1 tablespoon) soy sauce
pinch of salt

---

30 ml (2 tablespoons) beaten egg

Seasoning sauce for the squid:
45 ml (3 tablespoons) *dashi*
60 ml (4 tablespoons) soy sauce
45 ml (3 tablespoons) caster sugar
25 ml (1½ tablespoons) *sake*

---

5 ml (1 teaspoon) potato flour

Clean the squid as directed above. Cut the tentacles and flaps into very small pieces and dip in boiling water for 1 minute. Drain well. Soak the dried mushrooms in warm water for 30 minutes, then remove the hard stem and cut the cap into very thin shreds. Pour boiling water over the beancurd, drain for a few minutes, then squeeze dry in a cloth; it will now be in crumbs. Peel the carrot and cut into fine strips 3 cm (1 inch) long. Boil for 2 minutes in unsalted water, then drain. Par-boil the snow peas for about 3 minutes, then cut lengthways into very thin slices.

Put the carrots and mushrooms into the vegetable stock and simmer until the liquid is reduced by half. Add the beancurd crumbs and turn up the heat. Continue boiling and stirring until the mixture is dry, then add the chopped squid bits and the snow peas. The mixture must be really dry at this point. Stir in the beaten egg and mix briskly over the heat until the egg is set. Remove the pan from the heat and leave to cool. When cool enough to handle, stuff the squid sacs with the mixture, taking care not to fill them too full or they will split during cooking. Close the top openings securely with toothpicks.

Heat the squid seasoning sauce and gently boil the squid for 2–3 minutes, until they start to stiffen (larger-sized squid may require up to 5 minutes). Lift out immediately and leave to cool. Meanwhile, mix a paste of the potato flour and a little water and add this to the remaining squid seasoning sauce. Bring to the boil, stirring all the time. Cut the squid into rings and divide between four plates, spoon over a little of the thickened sauce and serve.

Deep-fried dishes

Tempura

Serves 4

The crisp, feather-light batter and fresh, delicate flavour of the fish and vegetables within make *tempura* one of the most popular Japanese dishes in the West. *Tempura* as it is known today is a comparatively 'new' dish, probably dating from the arrival of the Europeans in Japan during the sixteenth century. Deep-fried foods must have been familiar to the Japanese through their contacts with Chinese cooking from the seventh century onwards, but it was almost certainly the Portuguese who introduced batter. An earlier style of cooking in which deep-fried foods, without batter, are combined, or dipped, in a seasoning sauce can still be found in some modern Japanese simmered dishes.

Japanese batter, unlike Western batters, is not beaten in advance, but lightly mixed at the very last minute, so that the flour remains in lumps. The final lace-like texture of *tempura* comes from the uneven consistency of the batter. Any food to be fried in batter is always well drained and patted dry before being coated.

The Japanese use standard refined vegetable oil for deep frying, similar to that sold in Western supermarkets. It is most important to have clean, though not necessarily unused, oil. Oil is quickly tainted by over-cooked particles of food left behind, so it should be skimmed between each frying session, and, while still warm from cooking, filtered into a clean container. As soon as the oil becomes slightly cloudy or changes colour it should be changed.

Any deep, heavy saucepan may be used for deep frying. The depth of the oil should be at least double the thickness of the foods to be fried, but care should be taken not to fill the pan to more than half its depth. For a really light, crisp batter the oil must remain at a steady temperature of about 170°C (350°F). To avoid sudden drops in temperature only limited amounts of food should be put in at any one time. The temperature of the oil can be tested by letting a drop of batter fall into it: if the oil is at 170°C (350°F) it will hang between the bottom of the pan and the surface of the oil immediately it is put into the pan before rising to the surface. The oil is cooler (160°C, 325°F) if it drops to the bottom of the pan before rising, and hotter (190°C, 375°F) if it stays on the surface. Vegetables are best cooked at 160–170°C (325–350°F) while fish should be cooked at 170–180°C (340–360°F). An electric thermostatically controlled deep-fryer can be of enormous advantage in cooking *tempura*.

All deep-fried food should drain for a few seconds on a rack or absorbent paper; standard egg-and-flour-battered foods must be served as soon as possible after cooking, but fish or meat covered in egg and breadcrumbs or other coatings may be kept hot until all the portions have been cooked before being served.

8 raw prawns*
250 g (8 oz) dab or sole
300 g (10 oz) squid (body sac only)

———

Vegetables (3–4 of the following):
4 flat mushrooms, with central stalks removed and caps wiped clean
75 g (3 oz) pumpkin, peeled and cut into 1 cm ($\frac{1}{2}$ inch)-thick, bite-sized slices
50 g (2 oz) carrot, scraped and cut into 8 rectangles about 3 mm ($\frac{1}{10}$ inch) thick
1 large onion, cut into slices about 1 cm (1$\frac{1}{2}$ inch) thick, each slice speared with a toothpick to hold it together
50 g (2 oz) sweet potato, peeled thickly and cut into 1-cm ($\frac{1}{2}$-inch) rounds
75 g (3 oz) aubergine, cut lengthways into 8 thin segments
50 g (2 oz) french beans, trimmed to 5-cm (2-inch) lengths
50 g (2 oz) green pepper, de-seeded and cut into rectangles about 3 × 5 cm (1$\frac{1}{2}$ × 2 inches)
4 sprigs of parsley

———

Dipping sauce (tentsuyu *sauce*):
60 ml (4 tablespoons) grated white radish
20 ml (4 teaspoons) grated ginger
200 ml ($\frac{1}{3}$ pint) *dashi*
45 ml (3 tablespoons) *mirin*
45 ml (3 tablespoons) soy sauce

———

Batter:
1 egg
200 ml ($\frac{1}{3}$ pint) iced water
150 g (5 oz) plain flour

———

clean oil for deep frying

Thaw and shell the prawns, leaving on their tails. Cut along the centre back of each prawn and remove the black vein. Then gently press the prawns flat with the blade of a knife. Fillet the fish into four, and carefully skin each fillet (see page 45). Prepare the squid as directed on page 55. Slit open the body sac and score all over the *outside* surface in a criss-cross diamond pattern. Then cut into 4-cm (1$\frac{1}{2}$-inch) squares. Have the chosen vegetables prepared and arranged on a plate, ready for cooking.

* Raw prawns in the UK are grey, frozen, uncooked prawns.

Grate the white radish and squeeze dry in a clean cloth. Divide the pulp between four small shallow dishes, together with a separate small mound of grated ginger. Mix the *dashi*, *mirin* and soy sauce in a saucepan and bring just to the boil. Keep warm until required. While the oil is heating to 170°C (350°F) and after the diners have sat down, beat the egg well, stir in the iced water and finally sift in the flour. Mix lightly and use at once.

Dry the fish and vegetables and dip them, except for the french beans, parsley and mushrooms, one at a time into the batter so they are completely covered. Dip the french beans into the batter in bundles of 6–8 and coat only the undersides of the mushrooms and parsley in the batter.

Lift each piece of food straight from the batter into the oil. Put only small quantities of food into the oil at any one time: for example, either one person's helping, dropping the ingredients into the oil in the order of their cooking times, or all of one ingredient at the same time. After frying each batch, skim the loose bits of batter from the oil.

Serve the individual helpings arranged on a folded white paper napkin, spread on a small wicker basket or a plate. Give each diner a small bowl of warm dipping sauce together with one of the dishes of grated white radish and ginger so he or she can do his own seasoning.

An alternative batter to the standard one above can be made with 125 g (4 oz) plain flour and 300 ml (½ pint) iced water *including* an ice cube. When the oil is hot and the food prepared for frying, pour the water over the flour and, using chopsticks, make 3–4 deep cuts through the mixture. Dip each piece of fish or vegetable into the batter separately, coating completely, then drop at once into the hot oil.

Not all *tempura* need be coated in batter. Clean 8 raw prawns as directed above and trim off the tips of their tails. Dry the prawns well and dust with flour before dipping in lightly beaten egg white. Then roll in 25 g (1 oz) rice noodles cut into 1-cm (½-inch) lengths. After deep frying, leave to drain in a warm place until the rest of the frying is finished.

Other coatings for fried fish are black sesame seeds or powdered *nori*. Use four fillets of dab or sole cut into halves. Dry the fish with kitchen paper and dust lightly with potato flour. Then dip four pieces of the fish in beaten egg white and sprinkle 45 ml (3 tablespoons) black sesame seeds over them. Deep-fry at a moderate heat. Meanwhile dip the remaining pieces of fish in the beaten egg white and roll in 30 ml (2 tablespoons) powdered green *nori*. Deep-fry over a moderate heat and leave to dry in a warm place until the rest of the food is fried.

The foods cooked in these special coatings are not usually eaten with a dipping sauce – only salt. Note that by mixing the different types of coating it is possible to avoid a last-minute rush and cook the *tempura* at a more leisurely pace.

Vegetarian tempura

In Japan Buddhist vegetarians eat seafood and fish; so to the Japanese all *tempura* is basically vegetarian food. However, the two Buddhist recipes given below may take the place of fish and seafood in a *tempura* dish. Other Buddhist recipes appear in Chapter 5.

Leek fritters

Small leek fritters can be made to go with vegetables fried in a standard batter. When all the rest of the frying is completed, mix 100 g (4 oz) leeks cut into 1-cm (½-inch) slices with the remaining batter. Drop this mixture into the hot oil 15 ml (1 tablespoon) at a time, so it forms round cakes. Fry over a moderate heat and when golden brown lift out and drain.

The original recipe also suggests mixing in 15 ml (1 tablespoon) dried shrimps, previously soaked in hot water for 30 minutes and then well drained, for additional flavour.

Beancurd tempura

Serves 4

300 g (10 oz) cotton beancurd
15 ml (1 tablespoon) black fungus
60 ml (4 tablespoons) arrowroot or potato flour
15 ml (1 tablespoon) *sake*
25 ml (1½ tablespoons) beaten egg
30 ml (2 tablespoons) snow peas
oil for deep frying

Wrap the beancurd in a towel and leave to drain for 2 hours. Soak the black fungus in warm water for about 20 minutes, then rinse well and cut into thin slices. Mash the beancurd and mix in the arrowroot, *sake* and beaten egg. Blend very thoroughly and add the black fungus and snow peas, very finely chopped. Heat the deep fat to 165°C (325°F). Using an oiled tablespoon, shape the batter into small, flat cakes, or use the hands to shape into rounds about 2 cm (¾ inch) thick. Fry a few at a time for 7–8 minutes, then drain well. Skim the pan between each batch. Eat with *tempura* dipping sauce (see page 57).

Deep-fried breaded prawns

Serves 4

12 raw prawns*
1.5 ml (¼ teaspoon) salt
45 ml (3 tablespoons) flour
1 egg, beaten
50 g (2 oz) home-made breadcrumbs
oil for deep frying

Optional garnishes:
50 g (2 oz) white cabbage, very finely shredded
5 ml (1 teaspoon) *wasabi* mustard

Shell the prawns. Remove the centre vein but leave on the tails. Trim off the tip of each tail and sprinkle the prawns with the salt. Dry on kitchen paper, then dust lightly with the flour. Dip in the beaten egg, then in the breadcrumbs. Pat gently to ensure the coating is firm. Have ready the hot oil and deep-fry until the prawns are golden (about 4 minutes). Drain well and arrange on individual plates with a little of the shredded cabbage and a small dab of *wasabi* mustard. Serve with worcestershire sauce or soy sauce.

Slices of monkfish can be deep-fried in the same way as these prawns and served with a light sprinkling of *sansho* pepper.

Deep-fried char

Serves 4

Whole fish can be coated in egg and breadcrumbs before deep-frying. One of the most delicious is the delicate pink-fleshed char – a member of the trout family. In the UK char are caught in Lake Windermere during the summer, while in Japan they are found in Lake Towarda in the north of Honshu, where they are considered a special delicacy. It is said that the lake was stocked with these fish by a local *daimyo* (landowner) during the nineteenth century when he became appalled at the near-starvation of the peasants on his land. The fish caught in the lake today are descendants from his original stock.

4 small char
flour for dusting
2 eggs, beaten
150 g (5 oz) coarse breadcrumbs
oil for deep frying

Clean the fish as directed on page 43, leaving them whole. Pat dry with kitchen paper, then dust with flour. Dip into the beaten egg, then roll in the breadcrumbs until well coated. Pat gently to ensure the coating is firm, then slide into the hot oil, one at a time. Fry over a high heat until cooked (their eyes will puff out when they are ready), then drain and serve facing left on individual plates.

---

* Raw prawns in the UK are grey, frozen, uncooked prawns.

Meat

It was only just over a hundred years ago that a visitor to Japan reported that nowhere was there any animal meat on sale, and that the Japanese never ate meat. Nowadays most families in Japan expect to eat meat at least once a week, and many more often. However, some social constraints against meat seem to remain, particularly in its handling and retailing. During Edo times (1615–1854) a class of social outcasts were the only people working with dead animals – and, hence, with leather; according to Kaemphfer they combined this work with that of being public executioners. After the introduction of meat-eating in the 1860s butchering became an exclusive caste occupation for these people. At the end of the Second World War all forms of the caste system were officially abolished in Japan and butchery was no longer tied to caste.

However, the social inhibitions appear to linger on. Certainly Japan has no shops totally devoted to meat like Western butchers. Meat is sold in small grocers' shops, but from a partitioned area rather like a large cupboard at the back of the shop. Customers speak to the butcher through a small window set in a screen at about chest height. The various minced and sliced meats on sale are displayed very discreetly on small trays in tiny windows. The Japanese shopper is totally isolated from any contact with raw meat in its natural state.

In the supermarkets, where the greater part of all daily domestic shopping in the large towns is now done, the meat shelves display both pork and chicken minced with different proportions of fat, sliced and trimmed pork cutlets and fillet, boned belly of pork, and chicken joints, usually also boned. Beef is almost exclusively sold cut into thin steaks, at a prohibitively high price. Nowhere in Japan are joints of meat sold, as in the West, though it is possible to buy whole chickens in some supermarkets. Meat is always sold cut and trimmed ready for cooking. Tremendous care is taken over cleanliness in the handling of raw meat, not least because of the disciplines enforced on the community by the custom of eating raw meat and fish in *sashimi*.

The price of white meat is usually higher than that of most fish, and there is little difference in the prices of pork and chicken. The length of supermarket shelving for meat items is about one-third that used for fish.

Pork

Cold pork with a sour sauce

Serves 4

A very similar dish to this one is cooked in northern China: a piece of pork is simmered for several hours with ginger, onions, rice wine, salt and peppercorns, then allowed to cool in the cooking stock, which sets into a jelly; the pork is eaten cold, thinly sliced with the jelly, and served with a dipping sauce of soy sauce, vinegar and garlic. In the following recipe, as is usual in Japanese cuisine, the seasoning is added after the cooking is finished rather than during the cooking itself.

500 g (1 lb) lean pork, cut as a piece from the shoulder
1 small leek, washed and sliced
10 g (½ oz) ginger, bruised
2.5 ml (½ teaspoon) salt

———

Dipping sauce:
30 ml (2 tablespoons) rice vinegar
30 ml (2 tablespoons) lemon juice
60 ml (4 tablespoons) soy sauce
1 spring onion, finely chopped
1 dried chilli, finely chopped

———

75 g (3 oz) white radish
100 g (4 oz) cucumber
5 ml (1 teaspoon) salt

Blanch the pork in boiling water for 3 minutes, then discard that water and rinse the meat under cold running water. Put the meat in a pan and add sufficient fresh water to cover. Add the leek, bruised ginger and salt. Cover the pan and simmer over a moderate heat for 1 hour. Remove from the heat and leave to cool in the cooking liquor. Mix the dipping sauce and divide between four small bowls. Cut the white radish into matchsticks and leave to soak for 20 minutes in slightly salted cold water. Roll the cucumber in the salt, then rinse well and cut into similar-sized strips.

When the pork is cold, slice thinly and arrange the slices on four separate plates with the well-drained white radish and cucumber matchsticks. Serve with the dipping sauce.

Alternative dipping sauce for serving with cold pork:
30 ml (2 tablespoons) white sesame seeds, toasted
15 ml (1 tablespoon) *miso*
15 ml (1 tablespoon) soy sauce
7.5 ml (1½ teaspoons) caster sugar
25 ml (1½ tablespoons) *dashi*

Grind the toasted sesame seeds into a fine paste, then add all other ingredients and mix very well. Serve in small individual bowls.

Glazed pork with ginger

Serves 4

300 g (10 oz) lean pork

———

Marinade:
5 ml (1 teaspoon) ginger juice
15 ml (1 tablespoon) *sake*
30 ml (2 tablespoons) soy sauce

———

100 g (4 oz) white radish
5 ml (1 teaspoon) salt

———

Seasoning sauce for white radish:
30 ml (2 tablespoons) rice vinegar
15 ml (1 tablespoon) caster sugar
2.5 ml (½ teaspoon) salt

———

100 g (4 oz) snow peas or french beans
15 ml (1 tablespoon) soy sauce
5 ml (1 teaspoon) made English mustard
30 ml (2 tablespoons) oil
15 ml (1 tablespoon) ginger juice
15 ml (1 tablespoon) caster sugar
15 ml (1 tablespoon) soy sauce

Cut the pork into thin slices about 6 × 4 cm (2¼ × 1½ inches), and marinate for 20 minutes. Meanwhile cut the white radish into thin rectangles about 3 × 1 cm (1 × ½ inch). Sprinkle with the salt and leave for 5 minutes. Then knead with the hands until the radish becomes soft. Rinse well to remove the salt and squeeze dry. Mix into the seasoning sauce. Trim the snow peas and cook in boiling water until just tender. Then drain and cut diagonally into 3-cm (1-inch) lengths. Mix with the soy sauce and made mustard. Take the pork slices out of the marinade and shake gently to drain. Heat the frying-pan, then add the oil. Fry the pork slices over a high heat for about 4 minutes, turning to cook on both sides. Reduce the heat and cook for a further 2 minutes, then lift out the meat and keep warm. Wipe the pan clean and pour in the remaining marinade together with the ginger juice, sugar and soy sauce. Bring just to the boil over a moderate heat and add the meat. Continue cooking and shaking the pan until the meat is covered in the sauce and the pan is almost dry. Divide the meat between four heated serving plates and arrange portions of the white radish and cucumber on each.

Simmered pork and potato rolls

Serves 4

The ordinary potato is not a staple in Japan as it is in many Western countries, but a vegetable of the same standing as the carrot or turnip.

400 g (14 oz) soapy potatoes
300 g (10 oz) belly of pork, as a piece, boned
30 ml (2 tablespoons) oil
500 ml (¾ pint) *dashi*
30 ml (2 tablespoons) caster sugar
30 ml (2 tablespoons) *mirin*
pinch of salt
30 ml (2 tablespoons) soy sauce
40 g (1½ oz) carrots
40 g (1½ oz) runner or french beans

Peel and cut the potatoes into regular flat-sided oblongs, about 1½ × 4 cm (½ × 1½ inches). Put the pork in the freezing compartment of the refrigerator to stiffen, then cut into thin, bacon-like slices, 9 cm (3½ inches) long. Roll each piece of potato in a strip of pork and seal the loose end with a dab of flour. Spear each roll with a toothpick on the opposite side to that of the join. Heat a frying-pan with the oil and fry the rolls lightly until their colour has just changed. Transfer to a saucepan and pour the *dashi* over. Bring to the boil, skim, then cover with a drop lid. Cover the pan with an ordinary lid and simmer for 5 minutes. Add the sugar, *mirin*, salt and soy sauce, cover again and continue to cook until the potatoes are soft (about 20 minutes).

Meanwhile peel the carrots and cut them into batons about ½ × 5 cm (¼ × 2 inches). Top and tail the beans, and string if necessary. Par-boil both the carrots and the beans for 2 minutes in lightly salted water, then cool quickly under the cold tap. Cut the beans into 5-cm (2-inch) lengths. Add both the beans and carrots to the potato rolls for the last 5 minutes of cooking, and adjust the seasoning to taste. To serve, remove the toothpicks and put 2–3 rolls into each dish together with a few beans, some carrot and a very little sauce. Garnish with a little English mustard.

Tonkatsu

Serves 4

Tonkatsu are to the Japanese diet what fish and chips are to the British; always on the menu, they are served in restaurants of all social levels, while housewives can buy them ready-cooked to re-heat at home.

4 pork chops, about 150 g (5 oz) each
salt and pepper
flour
1 large egg, beaten
150 g (5 oz) home-made coarse breadcrumbs
oil for deep frying

Optional garnishes:
finely shredded cabbage leaves, lemon wedges, English made mustard

Cut the bones and the outer layer of fat from the chops. Season lightly with salt and pepper and leave for 10 minutes. Pat dry, dust with flour, then dip in the beaten egg. Coat with the breadcrumbs, pressing in well and shaking off any surplus. Heat the oil to 180°C (350°F) and deep-fry the chops, two at a time, for about 5 minutes. Then lower the heat and continue frying for another 3–4 minutes to ensure they are thoroughly cooked. Raise the temperature again for the last minute of cooking. Lift out carefully on to absorbent paper and keep warm while the remaining chops are cooking. When all the chops are cooked, cut into pieces approximately 2 cm (1 inch) wide and 5 cm (2 inches) long, taking great care not to dislodge the breadcrumb coat.

Serve on individual small plates garnished with shredded cabbage, lemon wedges and mustard, as desired. Often the Japanese also sprinkle worcestershire sauce over *tonkatsu*.

Chicken

Glazed chicken livers with spinach

Serves 4

250 g (8 oz) chicken livers
300 g (10 oz) fresh spinach or
 100 g (4 oz) frozen leaf spinach

Seasoning sauce:
30 ml (2 tablespoons) soy sauce
30 ml (2 tablespoons) *mirin*
15 ml (1 tablespoon) caster sugar

---

2 spring onions, cut into fine
 threads

Cut the chicken livers into bite-sized pieces, discarding any tough membranes. Blanch in boiling water for 1 minute, then drain. Wash and tear the central veins from the fresh spinach. Cook in a little fast-boiling water for about 6 minutes, then drain well and keep warm. (Boil frozen spinach for 2 minutes.) Bring the seasoning sauce almost to the boil in a small saucepan. Add the chicken livers and boil for 30 seconds, then lift out the livers and keep on one side while reducing the sauce to almost nothing over a low heat. Return the livers to the pan again and shake quickly to coat evenly in the remaining sauce. Serve on individual plates garnished with the onion threads and a portion of well-drained spinach.

Glazed chicken with poppy seeds

Serves 4

250 g (8 oz) chicken breast,
 without bones
5 ml (1 teaspoon) caster sugar
5 ml (1 teaspoon) soy sauce
30 ml (2 tablespoons) beaten egg
30 ml (2 tablespoons) plain flour

Seasoning sauce:
15 ml (1 tablespoon) caster sugar
15 ml (1 tablespoon) *mirin*
30 ml (2 tablespoons) soy sauce

---

5 ml (1 teaspoon) poppy seeds,
 toasted in a dry pan until they
 dance

Mince the chicken, then grind using a pestle and mortar or food processor. Beat in the sugar, soy sauce, beaten egg and flour until well blended. Bring 300 ml (½ pint) water to the boil in a saucepan. Shape the chicken paste into balls, the size of large marbles, by squeezing a handful of the paste up between the thumb and forefinger. As each 'ball' emerges, lift it off the top of the hand with a spoon and drop it gently into the boiling water. Make 16–20 balls in all. Boil gently for about 3 minutes, then add the seasoning sauce. Cover with a drop lid and boil over a moderate heat until the pan is almost dry (about 7 minutes). At this point remove the drop lid and shake the pan from time to time to coat the balls in the glaze. When well coated, remove from the heat. As soon as they are cool enough to handle quickly thread the balls on to thin wooden skewers. Allow 2–3 balls to each skewer. Serve on the skewers, sprinkled with the toasted poppy seeds.

Chicken simmered with winter vegetables

Serves 4

This is a traditional New Year's dish in Japan. It is arranged in decorative lacquer boxes and offered as refreshment to friends and relatives who come to visit at that time. The peas, a modern addition to the other vegetables, are for colour only and may be omitted. The original recipe was probably vegetarian, made without chicken.

4 dried mushrooms
75 g (3 oz) carrot
100 g (4 oz) canned lotus root
50 g (2 oz) canned bamboo shoot
150 g (5 oz) boned chicken leg
30 ml (2 tablespoons) frozen peas
25 ml (1½ tablespoons) oil

Simmering stock:
150 ml (¼ pint) *dashi*
30 ml (2 tablespoons) caster sugar
30 ml (2 tablespoons) soy sauce
30 ml (2 tablespoons) *sake*

Soak the mushrooms in warm water for 30 minutes, then discard their hard stems. Scrape the carrot and cut into flower-shaped slices about ½ cm (¼ inch) thick. Cut the lotus and bamboo shoots into wedges. Cut the chicken into bite-sized pieces. Dip the peas into boiling water for 1 minute and drain. Heat a saucepan with 7.5 ml (1½ teaspoons) oil and stir-fry the chicken until it turns white. Lift out and keep on one side. Add the rest of the oil and stir-fry the vegetables for about 4 minutes over a moderate heat. Return the meat to the pan and pour in the simmering stock. Scrape the bottom of the pan to mix in any meat juices adhering, taking care not to break the vegetables. Cover with a drop lid and simmer over a moderate heat until the pan is dry (about 50 minutes). Stir or shake the pan occasionally to make sure nothing is sticking to the bottom. Finally, just before serving, add the peas. This dish can be served either hot or cold.

Chicken tempura

Serves 4

300 g (10 oz) chicken breast, without bones

Marinade:
10 ml (2 teaspoons) caster sugar
15 ml (1 tablespoon) soy sauce
10 ml (2 teaspoons) *sake*

Batter:
45 ml (3 tablespoons) beaten egg
15 ml (1 tablespoon) soy sauce
15 ml (1 tablespoon) *sake*
30 ml (2 tablespoons) iced water
30 ml (2 tablespoons) very finely chopped leek
1 clove of garlic, crushed
70 ml (4½ tablespoons) plain flour
30 ml (2 tablespoons) potato flour

---

oil for deep frying
lightly boiled okra (optional garnish, see OKRA SALAD, page 117)

Cut the chicken into large bite-sized pieces and marinate for 10 minutes. Add the soy sauce, *sake* and water to the egg and beat together. Then add the leek and garlic and finally the flours. Mix gently. Drain the chicken and put into the batter. Heat the oil to 170°C (350°F) and deep-fry the chicken pieces, a few at a time. Skim the oil after frying each batch. Put the cooked chicken to drain on absorbent paper. Serve on four small plates, each covered with a folded paper napkin. Garnish, if desired, with a few slices of okra.

Chicken and nori rolls

Serves 4

150 g (5 oz) chicken breast, without bones
5 g (¼ oz) ginger, very finely shredded
pepper and salt
2 sheets of *nori*, 10 × 15 cm (4 × 6 inches)
oil for deep frying

Dipping sauce:
7.5 ml (1½ teaspoons) vinegar
7.5 ml (1½ teaspoons) soy sauce
7.5 ml (1½ teaspoons) *dashi*

---

finely sliced spring onion

Prick the chicken skin, then divide the breast in half lengthways. Slice across (not quite through) each half to open out into a piece double its size; do not let the pieces separate. Pat gently to flatten and scatter the shredded ginger over the pieces. Season with salt and pepper and roll up the chicken into two cylinders about 3 cm (1 inch) in diameter. Then roll each cylinder tightly in a sheet of *nori*, using a rolling mat (see diagram, page 74). Heat the deep fat to about 175°C (350°F) and fry the rolls for 7 minutes. Drain and cut obliquely into angled lengths about 4 cm (1½ inches) long. Arrange upright in four small dishes with a little finely chopped spring onion and the dipping sauce in a separate dish.

Chicken steamed in sake

Serves 4

300 g (10 oz) chicken breast, with skin

Marinade:
60 ml (4 tablespoons) *sake*
10 ml (2 teaspoons) soy sauce
1.5 ml (¼ teaspoon) salt

---

2 spring onions
12 g (½ oz) ginger
13 cm (5 inches) cucumber
10 ml (2 teaspoons) made *wasabi* mustard

Prick the chicken skin all over with a fork and marinate for 20 minutes. Chop the onions very finely and grate the ginger. Mix into the marinade, then steam the chicken in this marinade for 15–20 minutes or until cooked. Leave the chicken to cool in the cooking liquor, then, when cool enough to handle, cut into thin diagonal slices. Reserve the cooking liquor to serve as a dipping sauce. Meanwhile, cut the cucumber in half lengthways. Put a chopstick either side of one half-cucumber to act as a guard, and make a series of cuts down to the chopsticks at 2-mm (1/12-inch) intervals. Then cut the slashed cucumber in half lengthways and cut both pieces into 2-cm (¾-inch) lengths. Repeat with the second half of the cucumber. Arrange the slices of chicken on four separate plates and garnish with the pieces of cucumber and a little *wasabi* mustard. Serve the cooking liquor, skimmed of all fat and strained, as a dipping sauce.

Beef

Savoury beef squares

Serves 4

250 g (8 oz) lean minced beef
25 g (1 oz) leek, finely chopped
15 ml (1 tablespoon) finely chopped ginger
1 clove of garlic, crushed
45 ml (3 tablespoons) toasted sesame seeds (see page 167)
15 ml (1 tablespoon) soy sauce
15 ml (1 tablespoon) potato flour
pinch of pepper, or more (to taste)
10 ml (2 teaspoons) oil

Seasoning sauce:
200 ml (⅓ pint) water
30 ml (2 tablespoons) caster sugar
30 ml (2 tablespoons) *sake*
40 ml (2½ tablespoons) soy sauce

Mix the beef with the leeks, ginger and garlic. Chop 30 ml (2 tablespoons) of the sesame seeds until they are about half size, then mix into the beef. Add the soy sauce, potato flour and pepper and blend very thoroughly, beating the mixture against the sides of the bowl to expel the air (or use a food processor). Squeeze tightly into a ball and wrap loosely in cling-wrap. With a rolling-pin, roll the meat mixture into an oblong about 3 cm (1 inch) deep. Press gently to straighten the sides. Heat a large frying-pan with the oil. Remove the cling-wrap and fry the meat cake on one side over a high heat. When the first side is browned, turn it over, taking care not to break it, and continue frying on a lowered heat until the meat is cooked (about 10 minutes). Lift out and leave to cool. Then, using a very sharp knife, cut the meat into 3-cm (1-inch) cubes. Bring the seasoning sauce to the boil in a saucepan and add the meat cubes. Cover with a drop lid and simmer over a moderately high heat until almost all the liquid has gone (about 15 minutes). Watch that it does not burn. Finally, serve divided between four dishes and sprinkled with the remaining 15 ml (1 tablespoon) of sesame seeds.

One-pot dishes

The Japanese take particular delight in one-pot dishes, not just because it is fun watching food cook at the table, but also because the experience of sharing a pot is a novelty in itself. One-pot dishes are made with a wide range of ingredients and by various cooking methods, but the basic formula for serving them is the same. All the foods, either raw or par-boiled, and cut to the appropriate sizes, are arranged as decoratively as possible on several plates or baskets. Considerable trouble is taken over the presentation of the food, since much of the pleasure of this kind of meal lies in anticipation.

People tend to eat more at one-pot meals than at other meals, so the quantities should be generous. Allow about twice as much vegetable as meat. Quantities are suggested in the recipes, but they can be varied to suit individual tastes and pockets. The choice of vegetables can also be varied according to what is available at any particular time of year.

Put a free-standing gas or electric ring in the centre of the dining-table. Make sure that all your guests can reach easily into the casserole when it is standing on top. Give each diner a bowl of whatever dipping sauce is appropriate, and small dishes of any additional seasonings, together with a rice bowl, an empty bowl for the food and chopsticks. Have ready long wooden chopsticks to use for cooking and a ladle for serving the soup. A small wire scoop for retrieving food from the stock may prove useful if some diners are not very practised in handling chopsticks.

In the kitchen, bring the stock to the boil in the casserole, then transfer it to the gas or electric ring on the table; alternatively, bring it to the boil on the table while the diners are eating the other dishes.

When the stock is boiling, first put in some of the foods that take longest to cook, then add those that take less time. A certain skill is needed to judge in which order you add the ingredients so they will all be ready to serve at the same time. When the foods are cooked, invite your guests to help themselves from the pot. During the meal continuously re-fill the pot from the different plates of food, until everyone is satisfied. Then ladle out the stock as a soup to finish the meal.

A meal based on a one-pot dish need not necessarily include any other dishes except boiled rice and pickles. But for entertaining friends, or for a special meal, the pot can be preceded by a grilled dish or a salad (but not a simmered dish: in a sense many one-pot dishes are themselves simmered dishes). Nor is it necessary to serve soup, since the stock from the pot can be drunk as a soup. However, plain boiled rice is a must.

Salmon pot

Serves 4

Serve this delicately flavoured fish-pot, from Hokkaido in the far north of Japan, with grilled chicken and a salad, together with pickles and plain boiled rice.

700 g (1½ lb) salmon
180 g (6 oz) cotton beancurd
125 g (4 oz) *konnyaku*
8 dried mushrooms
250 g (8 oz) white radish
100 g (4 oz) carrot
250 g (8 oz) Chinese leaves
250 g (8 oz) edible chrysanthemum leaves, and/or fresh trimmed spinach, and/or watercress
250 g (8 oz) small leeks

Soup stock:
1500 ml (2½ pints) *dashi*
60 ml (4 tablespoons) white *miso*
15 ml (1 tablespoon) caster sugar
45 ml (3 tablespoons) *mirin*

---

seven-spice pepper

Scale the fish and cut into bite-sized pieces. Remove as many of the bones as possible. Cut the beancurd into 4-cm (1½-inch) cubes. Put the *konnyaku* into boiling water and boil for 3 minutes. Then place in a dry pan and allow to dry over a low heat for about 2 minutes. Cut it into 3 cm (1 inch)-wide strips, then make a slit down the middle of each strip and pull one end through the slit. This gives each piece of *konnyaku* the appearance of a plait. Soak the dried mushrooms in warm water for 30 minutes, then remove the hard stalks and cut a cross on the top of each cap. Peel and cut the white radish and carrot into half-moons about 1 cm (½ inch) thick. Par-boil separately until just soft. Put the white radish into rice water (see page 143) for the first 5 minutes, then change to plain water for the rest of the boiling. Wash the Chinese leaves and cut each leaf into 3-cm (1-inch) strips. Wash and cut the chrysanthemum (or spinach or watercress) into 5-cm (2-inch) lengths. Wash, trim and cut the leeks into angled slices about 1 cm (½ inch) thick. Mix the *miso*, sugar and *mirin* together and add the *dashi*.

Arrange the raw fish on one plate and the vegetables, beancurd and *konnyaku* on one or two other plates. Put the prepared stock into a casserole and bring it almost to boiling in the kitchen. Then, as the meal starts, bring the casserole to the table and put it on to a gas or electric ring. Immediately put in about one-third of the fish, white radish, carrot, *konnyaku* and mushrooms and allow to simmer while the diners are eating the other dishes. Then add a selection of the other ingredients and leave to cook for about 3 minutes. Never let the pot boil hard because the flavour of the *miso* would then be lost. Each person can serve himself from the pot, or the host can serve a helping to each bowl. Continue to fill up the pot until all the plates are empty, then afterwards serve the stock as a soup.

Shabu-shabu

Serves 4

The beef for this recipe, either topside or rump steak, should be cut into paper-thin slices (in Japan beef is sold ready-sliced for this dish). In the UK some butchers are prepared to cut it for you on their meat slicers; failing this stiffen the meat in the freezing compartment of the refrigerator, then slice it very thinly across the grain while stiff. When the meat starts to soften, return it to the refrigerator to stiffen again. Allow plenty of time for this job.

750 g (1½ lb) topside or rump steak, finely sliced
250 g (8 oz) cotton beancurd
8 dried mushrooms
2 large spring onions or 1 small leek
250 g (8 oz) Chinese leaves
150 g (5 oz) edible chrysanthemum leaves or fresh trimmed spinach or watercress
8 small button mushrooms
40 g (1½ oz) rice noodles
3 litres (5 pints) *dashi*
salt and soy sauce, to taste

Additional garnishes:
50 g (2 oz) spring onions, finely chopped
100 g (4 oz) white radish, peeled and grated
5 ml (1 teaspoon) finely chopped dried chilli

---

ponzu sauce (see overleaf)
sesame sauce or sesame and walnut sauce (see overleaf)

Cut the beef slices into pieces about 7 cm (3 inches) square, and the beancurd into cubes of 3 cm (1½ inches). Soak the dried mushrooms in warm water for 30 minutes, then rinse well and discard the hard stalks. Wash and trim the spring onions (or leek), and cut diagonally into 7-cm (3-inch) lengths. Wash the Chinese leaves and cut each into half lengthways, then into pieces about 5 cm (2 inches) long. Wash and cut the chrysanthemum leaves into 6-cm (2½-inch) lengths. Wipe the button mushrooms. Soak the rice noodles in hot water for 5 minutes, then drain well. Arrange the vegetables and beancurd with the meat on four individual plates to the best possible visual effect. Serve each diner with a plate of food, a small bowl of *ponzu* sauce (see below) and another of either sesame sauce or sesame and walnut sauce (see below). Also give each diner small dishes of chopped spring onion, grated white radish and chopped dried chillis. Allow diners to season their sauces as they wish.

Lightly season the *dashi* with salt and soy sauce to taste (remember it will boil down during the cooking, so take care not to over-salt). Bring to the boil in the casserole, then transfer to a gas or electric ring in the centre of the table. The diners each cook their own food by holding it in the boiling stock with their chopsticks. When each piece is cooked to their satisfaction they dip it in a sauce and eat it. When all the food is finished, ladle out the stock as a soup. Serve *shabu-shabu* with plain boiled rice, a small salad and pickles.

Ponzu sauce

Serves 4

30 ml (2 tablespoons) lemon juice
30 ml (2 tablespoons) rice vinegar
60 ml (4 tablespoons) soy sauce
50 ml (3½ tablespoons) *sake*
50 ml (3½ tablespoons) *mirin*
6 cm (3½ inches) *konbu*
15 ml (1 tablespoon) *hanakatsuo*

Mix all the ingredients together and leave overnight. The following day, strain through a clean fine cloth and keep close-covered in the refrigerator until required.

Sesame sauce

Serves 4

40 g (1½ oz) sesame seeds
100 ml (3½ fl oz) *dashi*
15 ml (1 tablespoon) soy sauce
30 ml (2 tablespoons) white *miso*
15 ml (1 tablespoon) *mirin*
15 ml (1 tablespoon) *sake*
7.5 ml (1½ teaspoons) caster sugar

Toast the sesame seeds in a dry pan until golden, then grind into a smooth, oily paste using either a pestle and mortar or a rolling-pin on a board. Mix with the rest of the ingredients. This sauce can be made well in advance of the meal.

Sesame and walnut sauce

Serves 4

50 g (2 oz) sesame seeds
15 g (½ oz) walnuts, shelled
45 ml (3 tablespoons) soy sauce
15 ml (1 tablespoon) *mirin*
30 ml (2 tablespoons) bitter orange juice or lemon juice
175 ml (6 fl oz) *dashi*

Toast the sesame seeds in a dry pan until golden. Then grind with the walnuts into an oily paste using either a pestle and mortar or a rolling-pin on a board. Mix with the rest of the ingredients. This sauce also can be made in advance of the meal.

Chicken and vegetable pot

Serves 4

1 kg (2 lb) whole chicken legs, with bones
1.5 litres (2½ pints) *dashi*, made with *konbu* only
5 ml (1 teaspoon) salt
4 dried mushrooms

Cabbage rolls:
4 leaves of Chinese leaves
100 g (4 oz) trimmed spinach leaves
75 g (3 oz) carrot

---

12 snow peas
2.5 ml (½ teaspoon) salt
40 g (1½ oz) rice noodles
75 g (3 oz) canned bamboo shoots
150 g (5 oz) cotton beancurd
180 g (6 oz) edible chrysanthemum leaves or fresh trimmed spinach or watercress
salt to taste
75 g (3 oz) grated white radish

---

ponzu sauce (see opposite)

Put the chicken legs into the boiling *dashi* together with 5 ml (1 teaspoon) salt. Skim well, then turn down the heat and simmer for 1 hour. Leave until cold enough to handle, then remove the bones carefully, leaving the meat in tidy, bite-sized pieces. Reserve the stock. Wash and soak the dried mushrooms in warm water for 30 minutes, then discard the hard stalks and cut the caps in halves.

To make the cabbage rolls, dip the Chinese leaves into boiling water for 1 minute, then pat dry. Boil the spinach leaves for 3 minutes in unsalted water, then refresh quickly in cold water and squeeze dry.

Peel and cut the carrot into batons 5 cm (2 inches) long × ½ cm (¼ inch) wide, then par-boil until just soft. Spread out the Chinese leaves on a rolling mat* so one overlaps with another and their stalks point alternately in opposite directions. Arrange the spinach in a layer along the centre of the cabbage leaves and lay the carrot batons in a line along the centre of the spinach. Then roll up the cabbage leaves using the rolling mat to get a firm, even roll, with the carrot in the centre surrounded by the spinach and enclosed in the cabbage leaves. Cut the roll into four 5-cm (2-inch) lengths.

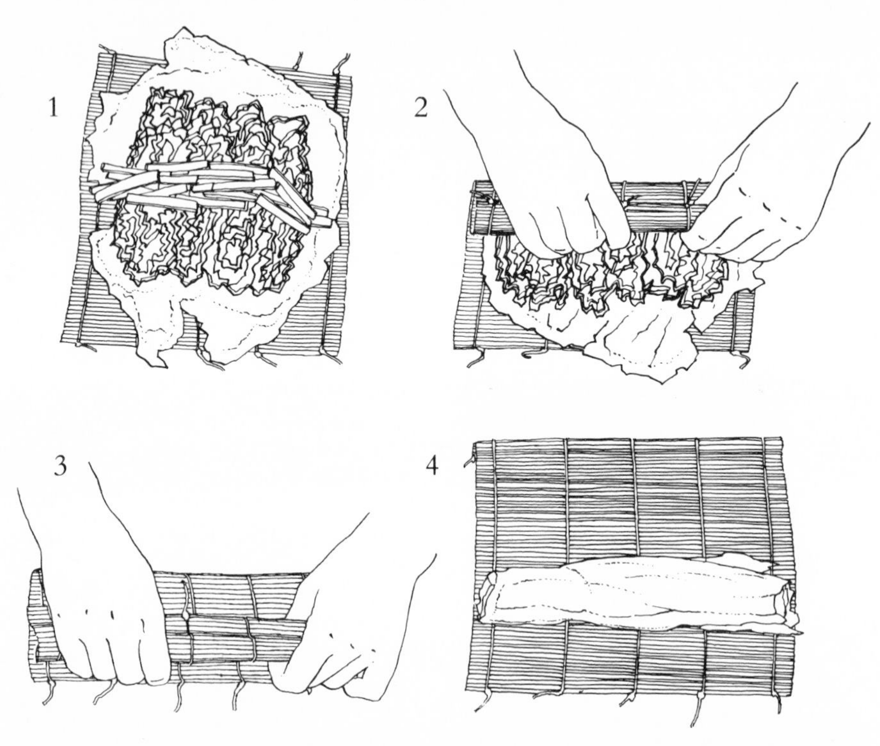

Rub the snow peas with 2.5 ml (½ teaspoon) salt, then rinse well. Put the rice noodles in hot water for 5 minutes to soften, then drain well. Cut the bamboo shoots into thin slices and par-boil for about 6 minutes. Drain well. Cut the beancurd into bite-sized cubes. Wash and cut the chrysanthemum leaves (or spinach or watercress) into 6-cm (2½-inch) lengths.

---

* The rolling mat is made from fine strips of bamboo bound together with cotton string, rather like a miniature sun-blind. It is used for rolling foods such as rice or vegetables inside a skin of *nori* or cabbage leaves, and helps achieve a tight, firm roll. These mats can be found in Japanese shops in London. As a substitute use a table-mat made of bamboo strips, or a doubled sheet of greaseproof paper (this is less satisfactory, however, since excess moisture cannot drain away).

Arrange all the prepared foods on several plates. Put the reserved stock into a casserole and mix in the grated white radish. Adjust the seasoning with salt. Put the *ponzu* sauce into four separate bowls.

When the meal begins put the casserole on a gas or electric ring on the table and bring the stock to the boil while the diners eat the other dishes. When the stock boils put in about one-third of the chicken, the cabbage rolls, bamboo shoots, mushrooms and snow peas and leave to cook for about 4 minutes. Then add some of the rice noodles, beancurd and chrysanthemum leaves and cook for another 2 minutes. Allow everyone to help themselves from the casserole or lift out a selection of the ingredients into each person's bowl. Continue re-filling the pot until all the food is cooked. Finally, ladle out the stock as a soup. Serve a grilled fish dish, a salad, plain boiled rice and pickles with this chicken pot.

Cod and Chinese cabbage

Serves 4

600 g (1¼ lb) cod fillet or steaks
8 dried mushrooms
3 large spring onions or small leeks
250 g (8 oz) Chinese leaves
250 g (8 oz) cotton beancurd
40 g (1½ oz) rice noodles
1.5 litres (2½ pints) *dashi*, made only with *konbu*

---

ponzu sauce (see page 72)

---

50 g (2 oz) spring onions, finely chopped
75 g (3 oz) white radish, stuck with 3 dried chillis and grated (see page 37)

Cut the fish into large bite-sized pieces. Soak the dried mushrooms in warm water for 30 minutes, then discard the hard stalks and cut a cross in the centre of each cap. Wash and cut the spring onions, or leeks into angled lengths about 6 cm (2½ inches) long. Wash the Chinese leaves and cut away some of the thickness from the base of each stalk. Then cut each leaf into three roughly equal triangular pieces. Cut the beancurd into 8 squares. Soak the rice noodles in hot water for 5 minutes, then drain.

Arrange all the foods on a large plate, or use several plates. Have the stock already hot in the casserole before the meal starts. Give each diner a small bowl of *ponzu* sauce, a dish of spring onions and another of grated radish and chilli as additional seasonings. Put the casserole on a gas or electric ring in the middle of the table and when the stock boils put in some of the fish, followed by the mushrooms and Chinese leaves. Finally, add some of the spring onion lengths, rice noodles and beancurd to the pot. When the foods are cooked invite each diner to help himself from the pot. During the meal continually re-fill the pot from the plate of foods. Finally, when all the food is finished, serve the stock as a soup.

Serve glazed pork or chicken as a separate dish in this meal, together with a small salad, plain boiled rice and pickles.

Mixed pot

Serves 4

This is a pot for a special meal since the ingredients, particularly the abalone, are expensive. Allow plenty of time for preparation and serve with grilled mackerel garnished with a vinegared turnip, a salad and plain boiled rice.

125 g (4 oz) edible chrysanthemum leaves or watercress
2 small leeks or large spring onions (see page 172)
250 g (8 oz) canned bamboo shoots
4 small yams
2 small white turnips
4 dried mushrooms
150 g (5 oz) cotton beancurd
4 cabbage rolls (see pages 73–4)
12 snow peas
2.5 ml (½ teaspoon) salt
12 canned ginko nuts
250 g (8 oz) Chinese leaves
50 g (2 oz) rice noodles

1 packet of *kamaboko* (with grilled edges if possible)
250 g (8 oz) chicken breast, without bones
4 large raw prawns*
250 g (8 oz) fillet of sea bass
1 can abalone (optional)

———

Stock:
1.5 litres (2½ pints) *dashi*
60 ml (4 tablespoons) soy sauce
30 ml (2 tablespoons) *mirin*
pinch of salt

———

seven-spice pepper

Wash the chrysanthemum leaves and cut the stalks into 5-cm (2-inch) lengths. Trim and wash the leeks; cut into 7-cm (3-inch) lengths, then cut each length into a brush by making numerous slashes at one end. Cut the bamboo shoots into thin half-moons and par-boil for 7 minutes. Then drain well. Scrape the yams and cut into regular bite-sized oval shapes. Rub with a little salt to reduce their stickiness, then rinse well. Put into plain cold water and bring to the boil. Boil for 5 minutes, then discard the water and rinse again. Bring back to the boil with fresh water and boil for 15 minutes, or until the yams start to soften, then drain well. Peel the turnips but if possible leave on about 2.5 cm (1 inch) of their bright green leaves. Put into a pan of rice water (see page 143) and bring to the boil. Boil for 5 minutes, then rinse well and cut into 2-cm (¾-inch) vertical slices. Soak the dried mushrooms in warm water for 30 minutes, then discard the hard stalks and cut a cross

---

* Raw prawns in the UK are grey, frozen, uncooked prawns.

in the centre of each cap. Put the beancurd into a dry frying-pan and brown gently over a low heat on both sides. Then cut into 3-cm (1-inch) cubes. Make four cabbage rolls (see page 73 and diagram, page 74). Wash, top and tail the snow peas and rub in the salt. Then rinse well. Drain the canned ginko nuts, rinse and thread on to four wooden cocktail sticks (three to each). Wash the Chinese leaves, and trim away the thickness at the base of each stalk. Then cut each leaf into three equal triangular-shaped pieces. Dip the rice noodles into hot water for 5 minutes to soften, then drain well. Cut the *kamaboko* into thin slices.

Cut the chicken breast into thin slices. Shell, de-vein and remove the heads of the prawns. Dip in lightly salted boiling water for 2 minutes. Pick out any bones from the fillet of sea bass, then, with the knife held obliquely to the fish, cut it into bite-sized pieces. Drain the canned abalone, rinse and cut into thin slices. Put the *dashi* into a casserole, bring to the boil and season with soy sauce, *mirin* and salt.

When the meal begins put the casserole of hot stock on to a gas or electric ring in the centre of the table. Give each diner a small dish of seven-spice pepper and an empty food bowl. While the diners eat the grilled mackerel start cooking the pot. First put in some of the chicken, then some of the bamboo shoots, Chinese leaves and mushrooms. Follow after about 4 minutes with some prawns, sea bass and cabbage rolls, together with leeks, yams, turnips and peas. Finally, add some of all the remaining ingredients. Try to stagger the additions to the pot so that they are all cooked at the same time without any being overcooked. Invite the diners to help themselves from the pot to a selection of the foods. Have ready the boiled rice to serve with the pot in separate rice bowls. Continue to re-fill the casserole until all the food is cooked. Finally, ladle the broth into the bowls so that it may be drunk as a soup.

Beancurd pot

Serves 4

This traditional pot is said to come originally from a Buddhist temple in Kyoto. It has become a favourite domestic winter dish.

12 cm (6 inches) *konbu*
pinch of salt

Seasoning sauce:
60 ml (4 tablespoons) soy sauce
15 ml (1 tablespoon) *mirin*
60 ml (4 tablespoons) *dashi*
15 ml (1 tablespoon) *hanakatsuo*

Seasonings:
20 ml (4 teaspoons) finely shredded spring onion
20 ml (4 teaspoons) grated ginger
60 ml (4 tablespoons) grated white radish and chilli (see page 37)

---

450 g (1 lb) cotton beancurd, cut into 8 squares

Wipe the *konbu* and make several deep cuts in its surface. Put into a large casserole about two-thirds full of cold water with a pinch of salt. Over a low heat slowly bring almost to the boil. In the meantime mix the ingredients for the seasoning sauce in a small pan, and bring to the boil. Remove from the heat and leave for about 3 minutes to allow the *hanakatsuo* flakes to settle. Then strain through a cloth and keep the sauce hot until required. Shred the onions, grate the ginger and the white radish and chilli and arrange in separate dishes for each diner. When the *konbu* stock is almost boiling slide in the beancurd and transfer the casserole to a gas or electric ring in the centre of the table. Keep at a low heat throughout so the stock does not boil. When the beancurd has heated through, lift out a portion of beancurd into each diner's dish and eat with the hot seasoning sauce and the seasonings to taste.

Sukiyaki (Tokyo-style)

Serves 4

600 g (1¼ lb) topside or rump steak
300 g (10 oz) cotton beancurd
12 flat mushrooms
75 g (3 oz) white leek, trimmed
1 medium-sized purple onion, or an ordinary onion
150 g (5 oz) canned *shiratake*
500 g (1 lb) green vegetables, e.g. edible chrysanthemum leaves, fresh spinach or watercress

---

Seasoning sauce:
75 ml (5 tablespoons) soy sauce
40 ml (2½ tablespoons) *sake*
40 ml (2½ tablespoons) *mirin*
75 ml (5 tablespoons) *dashi*
75 ml (5 tablespoons) caster sugar

---

1 chunk of good beef suet
4 eggs

Either ask the butcher to slice the beef on a bacon slicer, or stiffen the meat as a piece in the freezing compartment of the refrigerator and slice very finely across the grain. Cut each slice into pieces about 7 cm (3 inches) square. Wrap the beancurd in a cloth and press for 30 minutes, then toast on both sides in a dry frying-pan over a moderate heat. Cut into 3-cm (1-inch) cubes. Remove the stalks from the mushrooms and wipe the caps clean. Cut the white of the leeks into oblique slices about 1 cm (½ inch) thick. Slice the onion into thin slices, then separate into rings. Drain the *shiratake* and drop into boiling water for 2 minutes, then drain well. Wash and trim the green vegetables, removing any tough stalks from the chrysanthemum leaves and the central vein from the spinach leaves. Cut the watercress into short lengths. Mix the seasoning sauce in a jug. Arrange all the meat and vegetables in a basket (it is usual to arrange all the pieces of one ingredient together). Lay the table with chopsticks, a bowl, an egg and a rice bowl for each diner, and also some long wooden chopsticks for the cook. Stand a heavy frying-pan on a gas or electric ring in the centre of the table (it is better if the pan has no handle to get in the way of the diners). One person cooks the *sukiyaki* (usually the hostess in Japan, but others may take a turn). Rub the frying-pan with the suet. Start to cook by putting some pieces of meat, onion rings and mushrooms into the pan. Stir-fry continuously with the long chopsticks, and as soon as the meat changes colour add 2–3 tablespoons of the seasoning sauce to the pan. Continue stir-frying over a brisk heat, adding a selection of vegetables and more sauce to the pan. Meanwhile the diners each beat an egg in their bowls with their chopsticks. When some of the pieces of meat and vegetables are cooked the diners help themselves from the pan, immediately dipping the hot food in the beaten egg before eating it. Continue cooking fresh portions of meat and vegetables throughout the meal. *Sukiyaki* is usually served only with plain boiled rice and pickles.

Barbequed beef

Serves 4

This is a family dish in Japan, but because it is made with beef, which is expensive, it is eaten only occasionally. It may be accompanied by a clear soup and perhaps pickles as well as plain boiled rice, but often it is eaten as a meal on its own with only rice to accompany it. The piquant, tangy flavour of the dipping sauce is the particular attraction of the dish.

500 g (1 lb) beef steak, very thinly cut

Dipping sauce:
45 ml (3 tablespoons) soy sauce
45 ml (3 tablespoons) *mirin*
45 ml (3 tablespoons) *sake*
150 ml (¼ pint) *dashi* or water
15 ml (1 tablespoon) grated ginger
50 g (2 oz) onion, grated
75 g (3 oz) apple, grated
30 ml (2 tablespoons) sesame seeds, toasted and ground

---

2 large onions
300 g (10 oz) beansprouts
150 g (5 oz) carrot
12 snow peas
180 g (6 oz) green pepper
beef dripping
150 ml (¼ pint) *sake*, in a jug

Cut the beef into pieces no bigger than 10 cm (4 inches) square. Mix the ingredients for the dipping sauce in a pan and boil gently for 5 minutes. Allow to cool. Meanwhile prepare the rest of the vegetables. Cut the onions into slices 1 cm (½ inch) thick and spear each slice with a toothpick or cocktail stick. Pick over the beansprouts and rinse well. Peel and cut the carrot into thin oblong strips and top and tail the peas. De-seed and cut the pepper into oblongs about 3 × 5 cm (1 × 2 inches). Arrange all the food in a basket and put a little dipping sauce in each diner's bowl. Heat a large electric frying-pan standing in the centre of the table, or failing that an ordinary frying-pan on a gas or electric ring in the centre of the table. Grease the frying-pan with the dripping and start to stir-fry a selection of the foods. While they are cooking sprinkle with a little *sake* from the jug. As the food is cooked serve a portion to each diner, who dips the food in the sauce before eating it. Continue stir-frying and serving the foods throughout the meal. It is easier if only a small amount of food is put into the pan at any one time.

'As you like it' pancakes

Serves 4

Not all one-pot meals are main meals, as this recipe and the next demonstrate. This pancake recipe is for a winter lunch dish that is cooked in the centre of the table.

75 g (3 oz) Dutch white cabbage
75 g (3 oz) squid

Alternative fillings:
small pieces of octopus, dried shrimps, prawns, celery, or mushrooms
2 eggs
200 ml (⅓ pint) water
200 g (7 oz) flour
5 ml (1 teaspoon) baking powder
30 ml (2 tablespoons) oil

Seasonings:
worcestershire sauce, *hanakatsuo* flakes, powdered green *nori*, red pickled ginger

Cut the cabbage into hair-thin shreds and the squid into tiny morsels, almost as small as grains of rice. If using alternative fillings, cut into equally small pieces. Beat the eggs lightly and add the water. Then sift in the flour and baking powder and stir. Do not beat the batter: it should be a little lumpy. Heat an electric frying-pan in the centre of the table, or failing that use an ordinary frying-pan on a gas or electric ring in the centre of the table. The pan should be oiled. Have ready a small bowl and a ladle as well as the different seasonings. Put a ladleful of the batter into the bowl, mix in a portion of the cabbage and squid, then pour it into the hot oiled pan. Spread out the batter to make a pancake about 1 cm (½ inch) deep and 10 cm (4 inches) across. Sprinkle the top with a selection of the seasonings (each diner chooses his own) and cook until the bottom of the pancake is set firm. Then turn over and cook the other side. Finally, turn over once again and cook for another few seconds. Each person takes it in turn to cook his own pancakes.

Miso-oden

Serves 4

This hot savoury stew is a winter dish, made not only at home for supper but also in small bars where it is eaten as a hot snack to accompany *sake*. It is not cooked in front of the diners, but made in the kitchen and brought to the table steaming hot for everyone to help themselves. It is kept simmering on a centre table ring while the diners are eating other dishes. It can be served as either a snack supper or as a main meal. In the older districts of Tokyo during the winter, itinerant hawkers push little wooden handcarts with high wheels and curved roofs through the streets selling the hot *oden* stew.

250 g (8 oz) *konnyaku*
4 rolls of *kamaboko*
12 quails' eggs or 4 hens' eggs, size 6
200 g (7 oz) white radish
500 g (1 lb) small yams
250 g (8 oz) cotton beancurd
12 canned ginko nuts

Dipping sauce:
75 ml (5 tablespoons) red *miso*
60 ml (4 tablespoons) caster sugar
30 ml (2 tablespoons) *mirin*
30 ml (2 tablespoons) *sake*
45 ml (3 tablespoons) *dashi*

---

1 litre (1¾ pints) *konbu dashi*
cocktail sticks

Put the *konnyaku* into boiling water and boil for 2 minutes. Then dry in a dry pan over a low heat. Cut into lengths about 1 cm (½ inch) wide and 5 cm (2 inches) long. Spike the end of each piece with a cocktail stick. Cut the rolls of *kamaboko* at an oblique angle into halves and put a cocktail stick into the end of each piece. Hard-boil the eggs, then shell and thread on cocktail sticks (three to each stick). If using hens' eggs, hard-boil and shell, then put a cocktail stick into the pointed end of each. Peel the white radish and cut into half-moons 2 cm (¾ inch) thick. Put into rice water (see page 143) and boil for 5 minutes. Then discard the water, rinse and put into fresh water. Bring to the boil again and boil until soft (about 40 minutes). Then drain well and skewer each half-moon with a cocktail stick. Scrape the yams, cut into evenly shaped ovals and rub with a little salt to remove some of their stickiness. Rinse, put into cold water and bring to the boil. Boil for 5 minutes, then rinse again and change the water. Bring back to the boil and boil for 20 minutes, or until soft. Drain and attach a cocktail stick to each. Wrap the beancurd firmly in a towel for 30 minutes to dry, then grill in a dry frying-pan over a moderate heat until lightly browned on both sides. Cut into pieces the same size as the *konnyaku* and spear each with a cocktail stick. Drain the ginko nuts, rinse and thread three to a stick.

Mix the dipping sauce and stand in a pan of boiling water to warm through, but do not boil. Bring the *konbu dashi* to the boil in a large casserole and carefully arrange all the different ingredients in it with their cocktail sticks upright so they can be lifted out easily. Put the casserole on a gas or electric ring in the centre of the table and allow to simmer for at least 7 minutes to heat the foods through, before giving each diner a small bowl of warm *miso* sauce. Diners use their fingers to help themselves to the different foods, which they dip in the sauce before eating. Keep the pot simmering as long as people are eating.

Many alternative foods, such as meat, octopus, *aburage*, squid and different root vegetables, may be used in this pot, and there is considerable scope for invention. In some recipes for *oden* pots the ingredients are cooked in a stock flavoured with soy sauce, *mirin* and salt for perhaps an hour or more, and mustard is served instead of the *miso* dipping sauce for seasoning.

Small dishes

Small, or secondary, dishes in a Japanese meal are usually vegetable dishes, although they may include a little meat or fish for extra flavour and interest. They tend to be less elaborate in preparation and employ simpler styles of cooking, such as simmering, than those of main dishes. Garnishes, too, are much simpler for small dishes, perhaps limited to a sprig of green leaf or a sprinkling of shredded *nori* or *hanakatsuo* flakes.

Except in strict Buddhist vegetarian meals beancurd is rarely served as a main dish in modern Japan, but is regularly included in smaller dishes and in soup. Beancurd in Japan is an everyday ingredient, often mixed with meat or seafood and by no means a special vegetarian food.

Vegetables

A wider choice of fresh vegetables is commonly available in Japan than is normally the case in the UK, and the quality is almost always extremely high. However, it is possible to buy certain sufficiently similar vegetables in the UK to avoid any real problem in producing Japanese dishes. Some vegetables such as yams, sweet potatoes and pumpkins are more easily found in Indian and West Indian shops than in ordinary supermarkets, while others such as taro (January only) and lotus root can sometimes be bought fresh in large Chinese grocers. Edible chrysanthemum leaves can only be obtained by buying packets of the chrysanthemum seeds and growing them at home.

Some adaptations or omissions are inevitable when 'cooking Japanese' in the UK. One difficulty is the limited variety of fresh mushrooms in the UK compared with the wide range available in Japan: as a result, some dishes cannot be reproduced in the West. In other recipes, substitution is the answer: for example, salsify or scorzonera is suggested instead of the Japanese burdock, which is not usually obtainable fresh in the UK (all three belong to the same family).

Fried dishes

Spicy aubergines

Serves 4

450 g (1 lb) aubergines
75 ml (5 tablespoons) oil
5 ml (1 teaspoon) finely chopped ginger
30 ml (2 tablespoons) *sake*

Seasoning sauce:
45 ml (3 tablespoons) *miso*
25 ml (1½ tablespoons) caster sugar or more (to taste)
90 ml (6 tablespoons) water

---

5 ml (1 teaspoon) toasted white sesame seeds (see page 167)

Cut the aubergines into slices about 2 cm (¾ inch) thick, then cut each slice into quarters. Place in a bowl of cold water, and cover with a plate to keep below the surface. Soak for 20 minutes to remove bitterness. Then drain and pat dry. Heat the oil in a frying-pan and stir-fry the ginger for 15 seconds before adding the aubergine. Stir-fry for another 5 minutes over a moderate heat, then add the *sake* and seasoning sauce. Continue to stir-fry until all the aubergines are soft and the sauce is reduced. Serve in individual deep bowls sprinkled with toasted sesame seeds.

Stuffed aubergines

Serves 4

2 moderate-sized aubergines of about 200 g (7 oz)
50 g (2 oz) mushrooms
60 g (2½ oz) raw prawns*
2 eggs
pinch of salt
2.5 ml (½ teaspoon) *mirin*
75 ml (5 tablespoons) oil
30 ml (2 tablespoons) frozen peas

Seasoning sauce:
7.5 ml (1½ teaspoons) *mirin*
5 ml (1 teaspoon) soy sauce
1.5 ml (¼ teaspoon) salt

---

20 ml (4 teaspoons) cornflour
1 box of cress

Seasoned vinegar:
15 ml (1 tablespoon) rice vinegar
5 ml (1 teaspoon) caster sugar
1.5 ml (¼ teaspoon) salt

Wash and cut the stems off the aubergines. Cut each aubergine in half lengthways, then hollow out each half to make a boat-shape, leaving only a very thin shell. Reserve the hollowed-out pulp. Score the skin side of the shells lightly and soak both shells and pulp in cold water for 30 minutes to remove any bitterness. Wipe the mushrooms and chop finely with the aubergine pulp and the thawed and shelled prawns. Beat the eggs with a pinch of salt and 2.5 ml (½ teaspoon) *mirin*.

Heat a frying-pan with 15 ml (1 tablespoon) oil. Stir-fry the mushrooms, aubergines, prawns and peas for 2 minutes, then pour in the seasoning sauce. Add the beaten eggs and continue to stir-fry until the eggs are just set, then quickly remove from the heat.

Dry the aubergine shells and sprinkle the insides with the cornflour. Fill each hollow with the egg mixture, smoothing the top into a rounded mound. In a clean frying-pan heat 60 ml (4 tablespoons) oil and fry the stuffed aubergines, stuffing-side-down, until golden brown, then turn over and cover the pan with a lid. Cook over a moderate heat for another 5–6 minutes, until the aubergines are soft. Meanwhile trim the cress and sprinkle it with the seasoned vinegar. Serve an aubergine shell on each plate garnished with the vinegared cress.

Aubergines and peppers

Serves 4

100 g (4 oz) aubergine
50 g (2 oz) green pepper
25 ml (1½ tablespoons) oil, or more
15 ml (1 tablespoon) white *miso*
7.5 ml (1½ teaspoons) *sake*

---

* Raw prawns in the UK are grey, frozen, uncooked prawns.

Cut the aubergine into wedges and soak in cold water for 30 minutes. De-seed the pepper and cut into bite-sized pieces. Heat a frying-pan with the oil. Pat the aubergines dry and stir-fry until soft, adding more oil if necessary. Then add the peppers and continue stir-frying for another 2 minutes. Lift from the heat and stir in the *miso* and *sake*. Serve hot, divided between four small bowls.

Stir-fried carrots with sesame seeds

Serves 4

250 g (8 oz) carrots
25 ml (1½ tablespoons) oil
10 ml (2 teaspoons) caster sugar
15 ml (1 tablespoon) soy sauce
5 ml (1 teaspoon) toasted sesame seeds (see page 167)
1 dried chilli, finely chopped, or more (to taste)
15 ml (1 tablespoon) *mirin*

Peel and cut the carrots into matchsticks about 5 cm (2 inches) long. Heat the oil in a frying-pan and stir-fry the carrot sticks over a high heat until they start to soften. Add the sugar and soy sauce and continue to stir-fry for another 3 minutes. When the carrots are quite soft, mix in the sesame seeds and chopped chilli, and afterwards stir in the *mirin*. Remove from the heat and serve on individual dishes.

As an alternative, use 250 g (8 oz) scorzonera or salsify instead of the carrots. Peel and cut the scorzonera into matchsticks. Immediately plunge into cold acidulated water (15 ml/1 tablespoon lemon juice or vinegar to 600 ml/1 pint water) to prevent them turning brown. When the oil is hot, shake scorzonera dry and cook as above.

Simmered dishes

The stocks in which these dishes are cooked range from a simple *dashi* and *sake* stock to various carefully balanced combinations of sugar, or *mirin*, salt, soy sauce, *miso* and sometimes ginger. To obtain the best results from the various seasonings and to allow the flavour to build up properly *sake* is added first, then the sugar, or *mirin*, followed by the salt, vinegar, soy sauce and finally the *miso*. The order coincidentally follows the 's' sounds of the Japanese alphabet, so *sa, shi, su, se, so* are a mnemonic for *sake, sato* (sugar), *shio* (salt), *su* (vinegar) and *shoyu* (soy sauce). Some simmered dishes are served with a lot of liquid, but only the solid items are eaten: the liquid is left in the bowl. Such 'simmers' are served in dishes about the size of Western soup bowls. Other, smaller, bowls may be picked up after the solid food has been eaten and the small quantity of seasoned sauce remaining drunk straight from the bowl.

Simmered aubergines with a prawn sauce

Serves 4

450 g (1 lb) aubergine
10 g (½ oz) ginger
oil for frying

———

Simmering sauce for aubergine:
400 ml (⅔ pint) *dashi*
15 ml (1 tablespoon) *mirin*
5 ml (1 teaspoon) caster sugar
15 ml (1 tablespoon) soy sauce
1.5 ml (¼ teaspoon) salt

———

75 g (3 oz) pink prawns

———

Seasoning sauce for prawns:
30 ml (2 tablespoons) *sake*
100 ml (3½ fl oz) *dashi*
15 ml (1 tablespoon) *mirin*
5 ml (1 teaspoon) soy sauce
2.5 ml (½ teaspoon) salt

———

Thickening paste:
5 ml (1 teaspoon) potato flour
10 ml (2 teaspoons) water

———

sprigs of watercress (optional garnish)

Wash and trim the aubergines. Cut off three equally spaced full-length strips of skin from each aubergine, then cut the aubergine into rounds about 3 cm (1 inch) thick. Pierce the flesh of each round several times with a chopstick and soak in a bowl of cold water for 30 minutes to remove any bitterness. Grate the ginger and squeeze out the juice from the pulp.

Heat a frying-pan with about ½ cm (¼ inch) oil. Drain and dry the aubergine slices and fry on both sides until lightly browned. Lift out and drain. Bring the aubergine simmering sauce to the boil in a saucepan and add the aubergines. Simmer for 10 minutes. Meanwhile in another pan bring the seasoning sauce for the prawns to the boil. Add the thawed and drained prawns and the prepared ginger juice. Simmer for 5 minutes, then thicken with the potato-flour paste. Divide the aubergine slices, without their cooking liquor, into four small bowls. Spoon the prawns in their sauce over the top and garnish with a sprig of watercress. Serve hot.

Bamboo shoots with hanakatsuo

Serves 4

250 g (8 oz) canned bamboo shoots
300 ml (½ pint) *dashi*
25 ml (1½ tablespoons) caster sugar
1.5 ml (¼ teaspoon) salt
15 ml (1 tablespoon) soy sauce
30 ml (2 tablespoons) *hanakatsuo*

Cut the bamboo shoots into rounds about ¾ cm (¼ inch) thick and cut the pointed ends into quarters. Put into the *dashi* and bring to the boil. Then add the sugar, salt and soy sauce and simmer over a moderate heat for 20 minutes. Meanwhile put the *hanakatsuo* into a dry frying-pan and toast over a gentle heat until lightly browned. Tip into a fine cloth and crumble into powder. Towards the end of the cooking, the bamboo shoots will be almost dry, so during the last few minutes shake the pan to prevent sticking. When all the liquid has gone, add the *hanakatsuo* powder and mix in very well. Serve hot or cold in individual dishes.

Bamboo shoots with wakame seaweed

Serves 4

250 g (8 oz) canned bamboo shoots
25 g (1 oz) salted *wakame* or 1 length dried *wakame*
450 ml (¾ pint) *dashi*
25 ml (1½ tablespoons) caster sugar
1.5 ml (¼ teaspoon) salt
15 ml (1 tablespoon) soy sauce

Cut the bamboo shoots into rounds about ¾ cm (¼ inch) thick and cut the narrow pointed ends into quarters. Wash the *wakame* seaweed in cold water, then soak in cold water for 5 minutes. Remove the tough edge and cut into 4-cm (1½-inch) lengths. Put the bamboo shoots into a pan with 300 ml (½ pint) *dashi* and bring to the boil. Then add the sugar, salt and soy sauce and cover with a drop lid. Simmer for 20 minutes, then add the remaining 150 ml (¼ pint) *dashi*. Bring back to the boil and adjust the seasoning with soy sauce or salt. Add the *wakame* seaweed and cook for a further minute. Serve hot with the liquid in individual bowls.

Savoury red beans

Serves 4

150 g (5 oz) red haricot beans
1.5 ml (¼ teaspoon) bicarbonate of soda
60 ml (4 tablespoons) caster sugar
2.5 ml (½ teaspoon) salt
2.5 ml (½ teaspoon) soy sauce

Soak the beans overnight with the bicarbonate of soda in sufficient water to cover the beans well. The following day, put the beans on to cook in the soaking water and bring to the boil using a drop lid. Allow to boil for 3 minutes, then change the water by using the lid to hold back the beans while pouring out the old water and at the same time running in fresh cold water. When the water runs clear from the pan, return to the heat and bring to the boil. Boil again for another 3 minutes, then repeat the process of water-changing. This time, after the water boils, boil the beans until almost cooked (30–60 minutes, depending on their age). Then drain off most of the water, leaving only about 600 ml (1 pint) in the pan, and add 30 ml (2 tablespoons) sugar. Leave to simmer for 5 minutes, then add another 30 ml (2 tablespoons) sugar and the salt. Cook for another 7 minutes over a very low heat. If necessary add a drop more water. Finally, stir in the soy sauce and remove from the heat. Allow the beans to dry in the heat of the pan. (If there is any liquid remaining pour it away before drying the beans.) Serve in small bowls.

Stuffed Chinese leaves

Serves 4

8 good-sized Chinese cabbage leaves
75 g (3 oz) carrot
15 ml (1 tablespoon) oil
100 cm (40 inches) dried winter melon strips
200 ml ($\frac{1}{3}$ pint) *dashi*
15 ml (1 tablespoon) soy sauce
7.5 ml (1$\frac{1}{2}$ teaspoons) *mirin*
100 g (4 oz) minced chicken, 30% fat
5 ml (1 teaspoon) potato flour

Wash the Chinese cabbage leaves, then boil for 3 minutes until just soft. Drain well. Peel and cut the carrot into matchsticks. Heat a frying-pan with the oil and stir-fry the carrot sticks over a moderate heat for about 3 minutes, until soft but not browned. Rub Japanese winter melon strips with a little salt, rinse and soak in cold water for a few minutes, then boil for 10 minutes. (If using Chinese dried winter melon see page 173 for instructions.) Put the *dashi*, soy sauce and *mirin* into a small pan and bring to the boil. Add the minced chicken, stirring to break up any lumps, and simmer for 1 minute. Then strain out the chicken and reserve the stock.

Spread out the cabbage leaves to make one flat sheet across a rolling mat (see page 74), with the stalks at alternate ends. Sprinkle with potato flour and seal the overlapping edges of the leaves with a little of the flour. Put the carrot sticks along the middle two-thirds of the leaves, lying lengthwise. Then put the minced chicken on top over the centre third. Carefully roll up the leaves into a cigar shape, enclosing all the filling. Use the mat to make a firm, even roll. When it is a tight, firm package, tie with the melon strips at about 5-cm (2-inch) intervals along its length. Cut the roll in half and put both halves into a saucepan with the reserved stock. Cover with a drop lid and then the saucepan lid. Bring to the boil. Reduce the heat and simmer for 15 minutes. Baste from time to time with the sauce.

Before serving divide into four, and place each round upright in a small dish, with a little of the sauce spooned over it. It is easier to eat if each portion has also been cut into half.

Braised mushrooms with prawns

Serves 4

12 raw prawns*
12 flat mushrooms, about 5 cm (2 inches) across
36 small broad beans (frozen)
60 ml (4 tablespoons) *sake*
60 ml (4 tablespoons) *dashi*
7.5 ml ($1\frac{1}{2}$ teaspoons) caster sugar
15 ml (1 tablespoon) soy sauce
cornflour

Shell and de-vein the prawns, but leave on their tails. Wipe the mushrooms and remove their stalks. Boil the broad beans for about 3 minutes in lightly salted water, then drain and leave to cool. When cool enough to handle, remove their skins. Dust all the ingredients lightly with some cornflour held in a clean piece of cloth. Arrange a prawn on the top of each mushroom, and lay 3 broad beans beside each. Put the mushrooms into a pan large enough for them all to lie flat, and add the *sake*. Stand over a moderate heat until the *sake* starts to steam, then add the *dashi*, sugar and soy sauce. Cover and simmer over a low heat for 8–10 minutes, spooning the sauce over the prawns from time to time. Serve immediately in four individual dishes with all the remaining sauce poured over the mushrooms. This dish does not re-heat well.

The original Japanese recipe included cow-peas instead of broad beans; however, these are not available in the UK and broad beans make a tolerable substitute. In Japan on hot summer evenings bowls of plain boiled cow-peas are served for people to shell and eat while drinking, rather as nuts are eaten in the West. Shelled broad beans, boiled and cold, can be served as an alternative and skinned as they are eaten.

Sweet potatoes with mixed vegetables

Serves 4

Sweet potatoes were probably introduced into Japan at the end of the sixteenth century. They had been brought by the Spaniards from South America to the Philippines during the previous fifty years, and from there spread quickly to both Japan and China. Although they first became known in the UK at about the same time, it is only in recent years under the influence of the West Indian community that they have become a familiar vegetable in UK markets.

---

* Raw prawns in the UK are grey, frozen, uncooked prawns.

300 g (10 oz) purple-skinned sweet potato
25 g (1 oz) carrot
15 ml (1 tablespoon) black fungus
1 cake of *aburage*★
4 cm (1½ inches) *konnyaku* (optional)
30 ml (2 tablespoons) frozen peas

Seasoning sauce:
45 ml (3 tablespoons) *dashi*
7.5 ml (1½ teaspoons) caster sugar
7.5 ml (1½ teaspoons) soy sauce

2.5 ml (½ teaspoon) salt
2.5 ml (½ teaspoon) caster sugar
45 ml (3 tablespoons) *dashi*

Peel the sweet potato thickly and cut into pieces. Boil in unsalted water until soft (about 30 minutes). Meanwhile peel and cut the carrot into matchsticks and boil for 4 minutes in lightly salted water. Soak the black fungus in warm water for 20 minutes, then rinse well. Discard any hard bits and cut the fungus into thin strips. Pour boiling water over the *aburage* and slice into thin strips. Rub the *konnyaku* with a little salt, rinse well and boil for 2 minutes. Drain, cool and cut into thin strips. Dip the frozen peas in boiling water for 2 minutes, then drain.

Mix the seasoning sauce in a small saucepan and put in the black fungus, *konnyaku* and *aburage*. Bring to the boil over a high heat, then turn down the heat and boil gently until almost dry, stirring from time to time. When the sweet potatoes are cooked, mash them through a fine-mesh sieve and mix with the salt, sugar and *dashi*. Mix in all the other ingredients and serve piled in the centre of four small bowls. For the best visual effect do not let the food touch the sides of the bowls.

Braised pumpkin

Serves 4

Bright yellow-fleshed pumpkins are sold by the pound in West Indian markets in the UK during the autumn and early winter. They are not the same variety as the Japanese pumpkin: their skin tends to be more resistant to cooking while their flesh is softer. None the less, British pumpkins are perfectly suitable for this recipe.

450 g (1 lb) pumpkin
5 ml (1 teaspoon) salt
25 ml (1½ tablespoons) caster sugar
7.5 ml (1½ teaspoons) soy sauce
pinch of salt to taste

De-seed and wash the pumpkin. Cut into equal-sized pieces about 2 × 5 cm (1 × 2 inches), without removing the skin. Put into a saucepan of water with 5 ml (1 teaspoon) salt and bring to the boil. Boil until the

---

★*Aburage*: if unobtainable, substitute an omelette made with one egg, rolled while it is still warm and cut into thin strips.

pumpkin starts to soften (3–10 minutes, depending on variety). Drain off all but about a teacup of water and add the sugar, soy sauce and salt to taste. Cover and continue simmering over a low heat until the pumpkin is completely soft. Drain well before serving on individual plates.

White radish with miso dressing

Serves 4

In Japan, where the different seasons are clearly marked by seasonal foods, this is a winter dish – traditionally garnished with *yuzu*, a winter citrus fruit. However, at other times of the year lemon zest is substituted for *yuzu*, as it may be in the UK. Alternatively in the UK the zest of a Seville orange, if available, may be used.

450 g (1 lb) white radish
1 litre (1¾ pints) rice water (see page 143)

Sesame miso *sauce*:
7.5 ml (1½ teaspoons) toasted white sesame seeds*
25 ml (1½ tablespoons) white *miso*
10 ml (2 teaspoons) *sake*
10 ml (2 teaspoons) *mirin*
15 ml (1 tablespoon) caster sugar

Simple miso *sauce*:
10 ml (2 teaspoons) white *miso*
10 ml (2 teaspoons) red *miso*
10 ml (2 teaspoons) caster sugar
10 ml (2 teaspoons) *mirin*
10 ml (2 teaspoons) *sake*

---

zest of lemon to garnish

Peel and cut the white radish into 8 slices 2 cm (¾ inch) thick. Slash a cross in the centre top of each round and slightly bevel the edges, top and bottom: this will help them keep their shape. Put the slices into cold rice water, or add 15 ml (1 tablespoon) plain flour to the water, and bring to the boil. Boil for 5 minutes, but no more or the radish will become bitter. Drain and rinse well in clean water. Return to the pan with clean water, bring to the boil and boil gently until the radish is soft (about 45 minutes).

Meanwhile mix the sesame *miso* sauce. Grind the sesame seeds to an oily paste and mix with the other ingredients in a small pan. Heat the mixture until just below boiling point, then cook for 1½ minutes over a very low heat, stirring all the time. Take great care not to boil. Leave on one side to cool. Mix the simple *miso* sauce and cook in the same manner.

---

* Chinese sesame paste or Greek *tahina* paste can be substituted for the toasted sesame seeds, and although the flavour is not as good it will save a lot of time. To toast sesame seeds, see page 167.

When the radish is cooked, drain quickly and arrange two slices on each serving plate. Top them with the *miso* sauces, one of each on each plate. Garnish with either hair-like threads of lemon zest or four small oblongs of zest, slashed at each end and twisted into a triangle.

Simmered radish with chicken balls

Serves 4

600 g (1¼ lb) white radish
1 litre (1¾ pints) rice water (see page 143)
200 g (7 oz) minced chicken
40 ml (2½ tablespoons) *dashi*
10 ml (2 teaspoons) soy sauce
10 ml (2 teaspoons) *mirin*
10 ml (2 teaspoons) cornflour

Simmering stock:
600 ml (1 pint) *dashi*
30 ml (2 tablespoons) *sake*
25 ml (1½ tablespoons) caster sugar
30 ml (2 tablespoons) soy sauce

---

finely shredded ginger or zest of lemon threads to garnish

Peel the white radish and cut into slices 2½ cm (1 inch) thick. Slightly bevel the edges both top and bottom to help keep the round shape. Put the radish into cold rice water, or add 15 ml (1 tablespoon) plain flour to 1 litre (1¾ pints) cold water, and bring to the boil. Boil for 5 minutes, then drain and rinse well.

Mix the chicken with the *dashi*, soy sauce, *mirin* and cornflour and blend very thoroughly. Shape the mixture into small flat discs about 3 cm (1¼ inches) across and 1 cm (½ inch) deep. Heat the simmering stock in a saucepan just to boiling point and add the chicken balls. Continue simmering over a low heat and, as the chicken balls rise to the surface, lift out and reserve.

When all the balls are cooked put the radish slices into the stock and simmer for 45 minutes over a low heat. Then return the chicken balls and continue cooking for another 5 minutes. Adjust the seasoning with soy sauce and serve in individual bowls. Pour over all the remaining sauce and garnish with either shreds of ginger or lemon peel.

Yams in a chicken sauce

Serves 4

Of the world's many varieties of yams of different shapes and sizes, the most suitable for this dish is the Chinese yam (*Dioscorea batatas*), sold in West Indian shops in the UK under the name *edo*. It is the size of a small oval potato and is covered in a scaly, slightly fibrous skin.

450 g (1 lb) yams

Simmering stock for the yams:
300 ml (½ pint) *dashi*
30 ml (2 tablespoons) caster sugar
25 ml (1½ tablespoons) soy sauce
25 ml (1½ tablespoons) *mirin*
1.5 ml (¼ teaspoon) salt

---

75 g (3 oz) minced chicken

Simmering stock for the chicken:
100 ml (3½ fl oz) *dashi*
15 ml (1 tablespoon) caster sugar
30 ml (2 tablespoons) soy sauce

---

30 ml (2 tablespoons) frozen peas

Thickening paste:
7.5 ml (1½ teaspoons) potato flour
10 ml (2 teaspoons) water

Scrape the yams and cut into equal sizes with flat, regular sides. Rub with a little salt to remove stickiness and rinse well. Put into plain cold water and bring to the boil. Boil for 5 minutes, then rinse and change the water. Bring back to the boil and boil for 3 minutes. Drain and rinse again. Heat the simmering stock to boiling point and add the yams. Reduce the heat and simmer until soft (about 15 minutes).

Have ready the minced chicken and bring the chicken simmering stock to the boil. Lower the heat and add the chicken, making sure that the meat is well broken up. Continue to simmer for 5 minutes. Meanwhile dip the peas in boiling water for 1 minute, then drain. Thicken the chicken stock with the potato-flour paste and stir in the peas. Drain the yams and divide between four heated dishes, then spoon over the chicken, peas and sauce and serve hot.

A thousand grasses (steamed savoury custard)

Serves 4

50 g (2 oz) snow peas
3 dried mushrooms
40 g (1½ oz) carrot
100 g (4 oz) chicken scraps

Seasoning sauce:
45 ml (3 tablespoons) *sake*
15 ml (1 tablespoon) soy sauce
15 ml (1 tablespoon) *mirin*
1.5 ml (¼ teaspoon) salt

---

just over 300 ml (½ pint) *dashi*
2 beaten eggs

Wash and string the snow peas and cut lengthwise into very thin strips. Soak the dried mushrooms in warm water for 30 minutes, then remove the hard stalks and cut the caps into thin slices. Cut the carrot into fine matchsticks. Mince the chicken scraps. Mix the seasoning sauce in a saucepan and boil for a few seconds to burn off the alcohol. Pour in 300 ml ($\frac{1}{2}$ pint) *dashi* and add the vegetables and minced chicken. Bring to the boil. Cover the pan and simmer over a very low heat for about 8 minutes. Then cool immediately by standing the pan in a bowl of cold water. Drain off the liquid, make up to 300 ml ($\frac{1}{2}$ pint) with the extra *dashi* and add to the beaten eggs. When the chicken and vegetables are cold stir into the eggs. Divide the mixture between four deep, mug-shaped bowls and stand in a steamer. Cover and cook over boiling water for 15 minutes. Test with a skewer to make certain they are set. Serve hot in the bowls in which they were cooked. Eat with a spoon.

Steamed egg 'tofu'

Serves 4

The Japanese call this egg custard 'egg beancurd' (*tofu* is beancurd) because it resembles the squares of silk beancurd that are also often served cold with a simple sauce of *dashi*, soy sauce and *mirin*.

2 eggs
200 ml ($\frac{1}{3}$ pint) *dashi*
1.5 ml ($\frac{1}{4}$ teaspoon) salt
2.5 ml ($\frac{1}{2}$ teaspoon) *mirin*

Sauce:
75 ml (5 tablespoons) *dashi*
10 ml (2 teaspoons) soy sauce
pinch of salt
5 ml (1 teaspoon) *mirin*

Line a 1-lb loaf-tin with a doubled sheet of tinfoil so that when the egg custard is set it can be lifted from the tin without breaking. Beat the eggs with the *dashi*, salt and *mirin*, and strain into the lined loaf-tin. Remove any bubbles from the surface and put the tin in a steamer. Line the lid of the steamer with a wet cloth to prevent any steam from escaping. Steam for 2 minutes over fast-boiling water over a high heat, then reduce the heat and cook for 15 minutes or until the egg is set. Meanwhile boil the sauce for 1 minute, then cool quickly. When the egg is completely set, lift the tin from the steamer and leave until cold. Then gently lift the custard from the tin, and cut into 8 equal cubes. Arrange in individual small bowls and decorate with a leaf of watercress and a little *wasabi* mustard. Spoon over the sauce before serving.

Note The Japanese use an oblong straight-sided tin with a loose second bottom and narrow sides for cooking this custard, which makes it easy to lift out the cooked custard. The loaf-tin lined with tinfoil is a good substitute.

Beancurd

Beancurd, made from soya beans, is one of the most versatile of foods; it can be deep-fried or grilled, simmered or baked; its texture can be changed by freezing or re-formed by mashing and steaming. It is the richest source of vegetable protein, having half the protein content of meat or cheese, weight for weight, at a fraction of the cost. It is an ideal protein food for agricultural communities whose access to alternative protein sources such as meat or fish is limited, for whatever reasons. For nearly two thousand years beancurd has provided a large percentage of the protein in the diet of the Chinese peasants, and for over a thousand years it was a basic protein source for the largely vegetarian Japanese. In the West within the last forty years the value of beancurd as a food has begun to be recognized.

The Japanese people today are no longer living on the edge of malnutrition, and they can afford to eat expensive protein foods such as meat, but none the less beancurd remains one of the most important foods in modern Japan. This is partly on account of deeply ingrained vegetarian principles still generally current among the Japanese, and partly because of the qualities of beancurd as a food.

A firm pressed beancurd known as cotton beancurd is the most common and most versatile form. After the curding has taken place the whey is drained off and the curds lightly pressed into a cake. It is used for both frying and simmering, and for deep-frying to make aburage. Freeze-dried beancurd is also made from cotton beancurd. Unpressed silk beancurd has the whey and curds held together rather like junket. So delicate are the curds that they break almost as soon as they are touched. Silk beancurd is used for soups and in the summer it is eaten cold with various flavourings.

The residue left after the soya milk has been pressed out of the beans can be simmered with vegetables in a soy-sauce-and-sugar-based sauce; but more usually, both in China and Japan, the residue is used for feeding pigs. Skin which forms on the top of boiling soya milk can be lifted off and dried. This is a very common food in China, but in Japan it is found only in the old-fashioned traditional Kyoto cooking.

Beancurd-making

In Japan beancurd is no longer made at home, but either in factories producing large quantities of standardized beancurd for sale in the supermarkets, or in the small family businesses which are still to be found in most local communities. Very few beancurd-makers retain the traditional stove and hand-pressing but most still rely on skill and craftsmanship for the success of their product. Soya beans are converted into soya milk by a process of grinding, boiling and straining, and the resulting soya milk is mixed with a coagulant, *nigari* (magnesium chloride), to form beancurd. Family beancurd-makers grind the beans by machine and cook them under pressure. The milk is automatically separated from the bean residue at the turn of a lever, but then the traditional skills of mixing in the coagulant and transferring the curds to the cloth-lined draining boxes take over. The texture of beancurd should be quite smooth with no hint of graininess. The skill lies in distributing the *nigari* evenly throughout the soya milk without too much stirring or undue movement. A granular texture results from the curds being broken as they form or by their being inhibited from forming by too much movement; but equally, if the distribution of the *nigari* is uneven, parts of the soya milk will remain runny.

Work starts on beancurd-making at 5 am each day and finishes at about noon. Everyone involved wears gumboots and the stone floors are continually awash with water as the buckets and boxes are rinsed between the boilings. Large stainless steel baths of cold water hold the finished cakes of beancurd ready for the customers. When beancurd is made professionally the curd is drained in cloth-lined boxes with lids which can be weighted down to help the draining process. Such boxes are not available in the UK, although they are not difficult to construct (see below). In a Western kitchen the equipment for making beancurd is inevitably somewhat makeshift. The equipment described overleaf is that used by the authors for making beancurd in the UK.

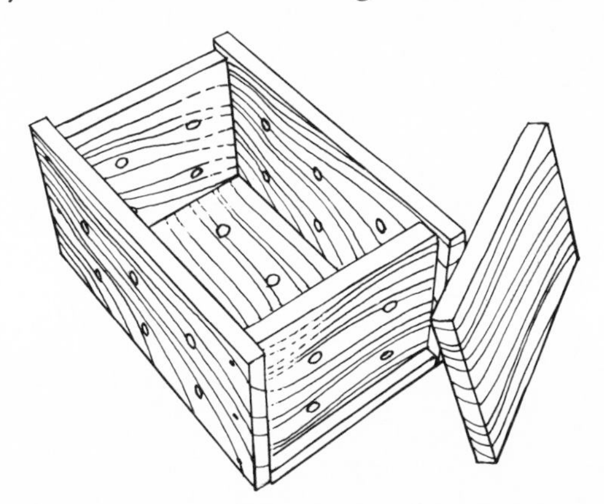

Nigari (magnesium chloride) comes in very small clear crystals rather like a coarse sea salt. It has no perceptible taste of its own, but the beancurd it makes has a delicate, slightly dry taste, noticeably different from Chinese beancurd, which is coagulated with gypsum (calcium sulphate). Magnesium chloride is difficult to obtain at the time of writing, but may be bought from scientific suppliers.

Cotton beancurd

Makes 450 g (1 lb)

250 g (8 oz) dry soya beans
2.1 litres (3½ pints) water
1.5 ml (¼ teaspoon) oil (optional)
5 ml (1 teaspoon) *nigari*
200 ml (⅓ pint) warm water

Equipment:
1 liquidizer
2 large heavy saucepans, one with a lid
1 wooden spoon
1 cotton bag or old pillowcase
1 measuring jug
1 jug with a good pouring spout
1 × 28-cm (11-inch) wooden-rimmed cook's sieve plus 1 × 20-cm (8-inch) basic springform tin, or 1 Japanese *tofu* draining-box (see page 97)
1 cotton teatowel
1 soup ladle

Soak the soya beans overnight in cold water. The following day drain well and grind in a liquidizer to a fine purée with 2.1 litres (3½ pints) water. (A liquidizer is better for this job than a food-processor, which tends to beat too many bubbles into the purée.) Put the purée into a large saucepan and cook over a high heat for 15 minutes, stirring all the time to ensure that it does not burn; reduce the heat when necessary. Remove from the heat and leave to cool sufficiently to handle easily. Pour the purée into the cloth bag and squeeze tightly over a clean pan to extract all the liquid. The liquid is now soya milk and the dry residue remaining in the bag can either be used for OKARA WITH VEGETABLES (page 100) or discarded.

Dissolve the *nigari* in 200 ml (⅓ pint) warm water in a jug with a good spout. Mix the oil into the soya milk (the oil is to help control the bubbles and may be omitted). Bring the soya milk to the boil, this time watching to see that it does not boil over. As it reaches boiling point stir with a wooden spoon. Lift from the heat and stir vigorously to create plenty of movement in the milk. Then slowly pour about half the *nigari* solution into the soya milk, criss-crossing the pan to distribute as widely as possible. Gently stir 2–3 times round the pan with the movement of the soya milk, then dribble in the rest of the *nigari* all over the surface of the pan but particularly round the edge. When all the *nigari* is finished, very gently stir twice more and cover the pan with a lid. Wait for one minute and stir round the outside edge of the pan once more to mix in the uncurded milk lying at the bottom. Cover again and leave for 6 minutes.

Place the sieve on the draining-board and stand the ring of the cake-tin, without its bottom, in the centre. Line the tin with the teatowel. If using a *tofu* draining-box, line with a teatowel. Using a ladle, lift off as much of the clear whey from the curds as possible and discard. Then very gently ladle the curds into the cloth-lined tin. Fold the teatowel over the top and cover with the loose cake-tin bottom. Leave until the whey has stopped running freely (about 5 minutes), then press with a 450-g (1-lb) weight for 5 minutes. Have ready a large bowl of cold water, remove the weight, then gently invert the sieve and slide the beancurd, still in the cake-tin, into the water. Remove the cake-tin and the cloth and leave the beancurd to soak for an hour.

Before using the beancurd, wrap it firmly in a towel to remove any excess water. If a firmer beancurd is required, press under a chopping-board while still wrapped in the towel. Home-made beancurd will keep for up to 5 days submerged in clean, cold water in a cool place. Change the water daily.

Simmered beancurd balls

Serves 4

300 g (10 oz) cotton beancurd
45 ml (3 tablespoons) *kudzu* or potato flour
20 g (¾ oz) carrot
20 g (¾ oz) broad beans
10 ml (2 teaspoons) black sesame seeds
pinch of salt

———

Simmering stock:
300 ml (½ pint) *dashi*
15 ml (1 tablespoon) caster sugar
30 ml (2 tablespoons) *sake*
45 ml (3 tablespoons) soy sauce

———

seven-spice pepper (optional)

Wrap the beancurd in a towel and press for 30 minutes. Then mash it with the *kudzu* flour until it is a smooth paste, leaving the sides of the bowl clean. Scrape the carrot and par-boil it and the broad beans for 4 minutes. After this chop the carrot very finely and skin and chop the beans similarly. Mix both into the beancurd with the sesame seeds. With oiled hands roll the beancurd paste into walnut-sized balls. Bring the stock to the boil and add the beancurd balls. Simmer for 7 minutes. Serve in individual bowls with a very little of the simmering stock. Sprinkle over a little seven-spice pepper to taste.

Okara with vegetables

Serves 4

Okara (beancurd residue) consists of the solid crumbs left after the soya milk has been squeezed out of the ground soya beans during the process of making beancurd (see page 98). In Japan it is either sold as *okara* or used to feed animals. The scorzonera or salsify in the recipe below has been substituted for burdock.

3 dried mushrooms
40 g (1½ oz) carrots
40 g (1½ oz) scorzonera or salsify
45 ml (3 tablespoons) frozen peas
200 g (6 oz) beancurd residue
15 ml (1 tablespoon) sesame oil
300 ml (½ pint) *dashi*
60 ml (4 tablespoons) caster sugar
5 ml (1 teaspoon) salt
7.5 ml (1½ teaspoons) *mirin*
15 ml (1 tablespoon) soy sauce
chilli pepper or seven-spice pepper (optional)

Soak the dried mushrooms in warm water for 30 minutes, then discard the hard stalks and cut the caps into minute pieces. Scrape and cut the carrots into similar-sized pieces. Scrape the scorzonera under water to help it keep its colour. After chopping it finely keep in acidulated water (15 ml/1 tablespoon lemon juice or vinegar to 600 ml/1 pint water) until required, then drain. If the beancurd residue has a strong smell, put it into boiling water and par-boil for 2 minutes. Then drain into a strainer covered with a clean cloth. Heat the sesame oil over a low heat and stir-fry the beancurd residue for about 1 minute. Then add the vegetables and continue stir-frying for another minute. Pour in the *dashi* and add the sugar, *mirin*, salt and soy sauce. Simmer for 20 minutes, or until almost dry. Serve hot in separate bowls sprinkled with the pepper.

Baked beancurd

Serves 4

300 g (10 oz) cotton beancurd
2 dried mushrooms
15 g (½ oz) snow peas

Simmering stock for vegetables:
25 ml (1½ tablespoons) *dashi*
2.5 ml (½ teaspoon) soy sauce
pinch of salt

1.5 ml (¼ teaspoon) caster sugar
2.5 ml (½ teaspoon) soy sauce
pinch of salt
5 ml (1 teaspoon) *sake*
1 small egg, beaten
2.5 ml (½ teaspoon) potato flour
100 g (4 oz) crab meat (see page 125 for dressing a fresh crab)

Seasoning sauce:
100 ml (3½ fl oz) *dashi*
7.5 ml (1½ teaspoons) caster sugar
1.5 ml (¼ teaspoon) salt
2.5 ml (½ teaspoon) soy sauce
5 ml (1 teaspoon) ginger juice

Thickening paste:
2.5 ml (½ teaspoon) potato flour
5 ml (1 teaspoon) water

---

grated ginger

Wrap the beancurd in a cloth and press for 30 minutes. Soak the dried mushrooms in warm water for 30 minutes, then discard the hard stalks and cut the caps into tiny pieces. Wash the snow peas and cut into minute pieces. Put both the peas and mushrooms into the simmering stock in a small saucepan and boil for 2 minutes. Then cool quickly.

Mash the beancurd and add the peas and mushrooms together with the sugar, soy sauce, salt, *sake*, beaten egg, potato flour and crab meat. Beat very well together to blend thoroughly. Line a 1-lb loaf-tin with oiled greaseproof paper and fill with the mixture, pressing well down and smoothing off the top. Stand in a tin of water and bake in a pre-heated oven (200°C, 400°F, Gas 6) for 30 minutes. Then leave to cool.

Just before serving mix the seasoning sauce in a pan and stir in the thickening paste. Bring to the boil, stirring all the time. Serve the cold beancurd cut into slices with the hot seasoning sauce poured over and garnished with a little grated ginger.

Toasted beancurd

Serves 4

300 g (10 oz) cotton beancurd
10 ml (2 teaspoons) oil

Seasoning sauce:
100 ml ($3\frac{1}{2}$ fl oz) water
15 ml (1 tablespoon) soy sauce
15 ml (1 tablespoon) *sake*
pinch of salt and sugar

Additional flavourings:
15 ml (1 tablespoon) grated ginger
15 ml (1 tablespoon) finely chopped spring onion
15 ml (1 tablespoon) *hanakatsuo*
15 ml (1 tablespoon) finely cut strips of *nori*

Wrap the beancurd tightly in a towel and leave to drain for 30 minutes. Then cut into oblongs about 6 × 3 cm ($2\frac{1}{2}$ × $1\frac{1}{2}$ inches). Heat a frying-pan with a good surface over a moderate heat. When hot, add the oil. Fry the beancurd gently to brown on both sides, turning only once. Lift out and leave to get cold. Mix the seasoning sauce in a pan and bring to the boil. Then leave to cool. Prepare the additional flavourings and arrange a pile of each on four small plates. Serve the beancurd in individual dishes with the seasoning sauce poured over it.

Summer beancurd

On hot evenings in the summer the Japanese often eat cold drained beancurd that has not been toasted. They use the same seasoning sauce as is used for toasted beancurd and flavour it with grated ginger, finely chopped spring onions, *hanakatsuo* and strips of *nori*, or they may eat it with slivers of garlic, seven-spice pepper or *wasabi* mustard.

Fried beancurd

Serves 4

The changing seasons of the year are clearly marked in the recipes for fried beancurd. Both start from the same point, but in the hot summer it is served cold with chilli-hot seasonings, while for the winter it is served hot in a savoury sauce.

300 g (10 oz) cotton beancurd
15 ml (1 tablespoon) *kudzu* or potato flour
clean oil for deep frying

Wrap and press the beancurd until well drained. Then cut into 12 equal-sized cubes. Pat dry and dust very lightly with the flour. Heat the oil to 165°C (325°F) and fry the beancurd over a low heat until the colour has just changed. Lift out and drain.

Summer fried beancurd

Dipping sauce:
100 ml (3½ fl oz) *dashi*
5 ml (1 teaspoon) *mirin*
30 ml (2 tablespoons) soy sauce

---

40 g (1½ oz) white radish
1 large dried chilli
chilli pepper or finely chopped dried chilli, to taste

Mix the dipping sauce in a small saucepan and bring to the boil. Then remove from the heat and allow to cool.

Peel the white radish and make a hole through the centre with a chopstick. Insert the chilli into the hole and grate both radish and chilli together. Squeeze the pulp dry in a clean cloth. This paste is called, rather romantically, 'autumn leaves'.

Serve the cold fried beancurd cubes on individual plates garnished with a small mound of white radish and chilli and with the dipping sauce in a small bowl at the side. Sprinkle the beancurd with a little chilli pepper or finely chopped dried chilli for a hotter seasoning.

Winter fried beancurd

Seasoning sauce:
200 ml (⅓ pint) *dashi*
10 ml (2 teaspoons) *mirin*
45 ml (3 tablespoons) soy sauce
pinch of salt

---

200 g (7 oz) white radish
red ginger shreds

Mix the seasoning sauce in a pan. Peel and grate the white radish. Squeeze the pulp dry in a clean cloth and add to the seasoning sauce.

Bring the sauce almost to boiling point and slide in the fried beancurd cubes. Simmer for a few moments to heat through, then serve in individual bowls with the seasoning sauce. Decorate with shreds of red pickled ginger.

Braised beancurd in milk

Serves 4

300 g (10 oz) beancurd, in 4 cakes
450 ml (¾ pint) milk
5 ml (1 teaspoon) soy sauce
1 chicken stock cube
2.5 ml (½ teaspoon) ginger juice

Thickening paste:
10 ml (2 teaspoons) potato flour
15 ml (1 tablespoon) water

Garnish:
12 g (½ oz) *wakame* (for preparation see page 165)
grated ginger
2 spring onions, finely chopped

Drain the beancurd and put the cakes carefully into a saucepan. Add the milk, soy sauce, stock cube and ginger juice. Put over a moderate heat, and bring slowly to the boil. Make sure the stock cube dissolves completely. Lift from the heat and spoon in the thickening paste around the sides of the pan. Bring back to a gentle boil to thicken the sauce, stirring carefully so as not to break the beancurd squares. Lift each square into an individual bowl, pour the sauce over and garnish with thin shreds of the *wakame*, grated ginger and the finely chopped onion to taste.

Braised frozen beancurd

Serves 4

Beancurd does not keep long in its natural state. Early in its history the northern Chinese discovered that by putting the beancurd outside and freezing it they were able to keep it for weeks during the winter months. Moreover the de-naturing that took place in the freezing process produced an interesting new texture – always an important element in Chinese cooking. The Japanese learned this technique from the Chinese and it became the standard winter treatment for beancurd in Japan. Nowadays it is not sold ready-frozen but housewives sometimes buy cotton beancurd and leave it in the freezing compartment of the refrigerator overnight. Because of its origins frozen beancurd is regarded as a winter dish in Japan.

300 g (10 oz) cotton beancurd
20 snow peas or french beans
75 g (3 oz) carrot

7.5 ml (1½ teaspoons) soy sauce
7.5 ml (1½ teaspoons) *mirin*
pinch of salt

Simmering stock:
300 ml (½ pint) *dashi*
25 ml (1½ tablespoons) caster sugar

3-cm (1-inch) square *konbu* (optional)
yuzu peel

Wrap the beancurd firmly in a towel and press for at least 30 minutes. Then leave in the freezing compartment of the refrigerator overnight. The following day thaw in a bowl of hot water. When completely soft, gently press out the water and cut into 5-cm (2-inch) squares. Cut the peas into halves diagonally. Peel and cut the carrot into ½-cm (¼-inch) flower-shaped slices (see page 28). Cook the peas and carrots in lightly salted boiling water until just tender (about 5 minutes), then rinse in cold water and drain well. Put the simmering stock into a saucepan with the *konbu* and bring almost to the boil. Add the beancurd and simmer, without a lid, for about 20 minutes. If using *konbu* take great care not to let it boil. Add the peas and beans and cook for another minute. Then serve in deep bowls with all the sauce, garnished with 4–5 thin shreds of *yuzu* peel. The zest of a Seville orange or a lemon may be substituted for *yuzu* if necessary.

Freeze-dried beancurd with vegetables

Serves 4

The development of dried frozen beancurd from the Chinese frozen beancurd was uniquely Japanese. The great advantage of this kind of beancurd is that it can be kept for long periods of time without continual freezing. The method of drying as well as freezing was invented by Buddhist monks at the Koya monastery near Kyoto at some time during the thirteenth century. Beancurd subjected to this treatment could easily be stored and transported to all parts of Japan, even during the summer. By the seventeenth century freeze-dried beancurd was a standard food, not just for the Buddhist monks but for all Japanese people, as it is to this day.

The recipe below is for a strict Buddhist vegetarian dish, belonging to the classical style with which the tea ceremony is also associated, marked by the simplicity and naturalness of the flavours of the different ingredients. Part of its appeal lies in the presentation, in which the juxtaposition of colour and shape plays a major rôle. Each element of the dish is cooked separately, to be united only in the final serving. All the *dashi* used in this dish should be made with *konbu* alone, without the addition of *hanakatsuo*.

2 blocks freeze-dried beancurd

———

Simmering stock for beancurd:
200 ml ($\frac{1}{3}$ pint) *dashi*
2.5 ml ($\frac{1}{2}$ teaspoon) salt
3.5 ml ($\frac{3}{4}$ teaspoon) soy sauce
30 ml (2 tablespoons) caster sugar

———

8 small dried mushrooms

———

Simmering stock for mushrooms:
100 ml ($3\frac{1}{2}$ fl oz) mushroom soaking water
15 ml (1 tablespoon) caster sugar
15 ml (1 tablespoon) *mirin*
15 ml (1 tablespoon) soy sauce

———

100 g (4 oz) carrots

———

Simmering stock for carrots:
200 ml ($\frac{1}{3}$ pint) *dashi*
pinch of salt
10 ml (2 teaspoons) caster sugar
1.5 ml ($\frac{1}{4}$ teaspoon) soy sauce

———

12 snow peas or french beans

———

Simmering stock for snow peas:
45 ml (3 tablespoons) *dashi*
pinch of salt
5 ml (1 teaspoon) caster sugar
1.5 ml ($\frac{1}{4}$ teaspoon) soy sauce

———

250 g (8 oz) packet of *konnyaku* (optional)

———

Simmering stock for konnyaku:
200 ml ($\frac{1}{3}$ pint) *dashi*
15 ml (1 tablespoon) soy sauce
10 ml (2 teaspoons) sugar
30 ml (2 tablespoons) *sake*

Soften the beancurd in hand-hot water for about 10 minutes, then squeeze dry. Bring the beancurd simmering stock to the boil and put in the beancurd squares. Simmer for 10–15 minutes. Then remove the pan from the heat and leave the beancurd in the stock until required. Wash and soak the dried mushrooms for 30 minutes in 150 ml ($\frac{1}{4}$ pint) warm water. Discard the hard stems and simmer the caps with 100 ml ($3\frac{1}{2}$ fl oz) of the soaking water together with the sugar, *mirin* and soy sauce for 5 minutes. Keep hot in the simmering stock until required. Scrape the carrots and cut into flower-shaped slices about 1 cm ($\frac{1}{2}$ inch) thick. Boil in plain water for 3–4 minutes, then transfer to the carrot simmering stock. Simmer until soft (about 15 minutes), then keep hot in the stock until required. Trim the tops of the snow peas or french beans and remove any tough strings. Cut a V out of each end and boil in lightly salted water for 2–3 minutes (if using french beans, 5 minutes). Then drain and transfer to the hot simmering stock and simmer for 1 minute. Remove from the heat and leave in the stock until required. Cut the *konnyaku* into slices 1 cm ($\frac{1}{2}$ inch) thick and 8 cm ($3\frac{1}{2}$ inches) long. Make a slit in the centre of each and draw one end through the slit, putting a twist into the sides of the oblong. Dip into boiling water for 2–3 minutes, then transfer to a dry pan and over a moderate heat dry the *konnyaku* for 1–2 minutes. Heat the simmering stock, add the *konnyaku* and simmer for 10 minutes.

Serve by draining the beancurd and cutting each cake into six. Arrange three cubes on each serving plate, together with 3 snow peas, a piece of *konnyaku*, 2 mushrooms and about 3 carrot flowers. Do not spoon out any of the cooking liquor, since this dish should be dry except for the liquid trapped in the vegetables. It need not be served piping hot.

Aburage

Commercially produced frozen *aburage* from Japan can be bought in Japanese foodshops in the UK.

300 g (10 oz) cotton beancurd, home-made or bought*
clean oil for frying

Wrap the beancurd tightly in a cloth and leave to drain for 30 minutes. Then cut into horizontal slices about $\frac{3}{4}$ cm ($\frac{1}{4}$ inch) thick. Heat $1\frac{1}{2}$ cm ($\frac{1}{2}$ inch) oil in a large saucepan to 30°C (85°F, blood heat) over a moderate heat. (A cooking thermometer is useful for this dish.) Slide in 1–2 slices of beancurd: there must be enough room for them to lie flat on the bottom of the pan without any overlap. Continue cooking over moderate heat, bringing the oil temperature up to 180°C (350°F) within 8–9 minutes. Turn the slices after 6 minutes, when they have risen to the surface. When the temperature reaches 180°C (350°F) lift out the beancurd and leave to drain. Cool the oil to blood heat before starting to fry again.

If the oil heats too slowly the skin of the beancurd will become tough and leathery, but if the heat is too high and the beancurd cooks too quickly it will not be cooked through and will remain wet and heavy. If it cooks too long it will lose its delicate texture and become hard.

* Chinese commerically made beancurd is not suitable for making *aburage*.

Aburage rolls with beancurd and chicken

Serves 4

The chicken may be omitted from this dish, in which case increase the number of snow peas by one-third.

4 cakes of *aburage*, 14 × 5 cm (5½ × 3½ inches)
100 cm (40 inches) dried winter melon strips
12 snow peas or french beans

Simmering stock for peas:
200 ml (⅓ pint) *dashi*
10 ml (2 teaspoons) caster sugar
1.5 ml (¼ teaspoon) salt
15 ml (1 tablespoon) *mirin*

---

100 g (4 oz) chicken meat, without bones
300 g (10 oz) cotton beancurd
5 ml (1 teaspoon) caster sugar
2.5 ml (½ teaspoon) salt

Seasoning sauce:
400 ml (⅔ pint) *dashi*
45 ml (3 tablespoons) caster sugar
30 ml (2 tablespoons) soy sauce
1.5 ml (¼ teaspoon) salt
30 ml (2 tablespoons) *mirin*
30 ml (2 tablespoons) *sake*

Pour boiling water over the *aburage* to remove any oiliness, then pat dry. Trim off one long edge and the two narrow edges from each cake. Carefully open out each *aburage* cake into one flat sheet double its original size and hinged at the remaining side edge, forming approximately a 15-cm (6-inch) square. Trim the snow peas, blanch in boiling lightly salted water for 1 minute, then simmer in the stock until tender (about 4 minutes). Drain well. Rinse the dried winter melon strips and rub with a little salt between the hands. Then rinse well and boil for 10 minutes to soften. (If using Chinese winter melon strips see page 173.) Mince the chicken very finely, using a mincer or a food processor. Dip the beancurd square into boiling water for 30 seconds, then drain well and mash with a fork. Mix the mashed beancurd with the chicken and season with sugar and salt. (A food processor can be used for making the beancurd and chicken paste.) Spread one-quarter of the chicken paste over one sheet of *aburage*, leaving a strip at one end about 5 cm (1½ inches) wide without the paste. Lay 3 snow peas across the middle of the chicken paste, then roll the *aburage* and chicken round the peas into a firm, cigar-shaped cylinder, finishing with the strip of uncoated *aburage*. Tie the roll securely in three places with the winter melon strips, or use toothpicks. Repeat with the remaining sheets of *aburage*. Put the rolls in a saucepan with the seasoning sauce and simmer gently for 30 minutes. The sauce should be reduced to one-third. Cut each roll into three. Serve in individual deep bowls with the sauce poured over the rolls.

Aburage egg pouches

Serves 4

2 large cakes *aburage*, 14 × 9 cm (5½ × 3½ inches), or 4 small ones
4 small eggs, size 6
80 cm (32 inches) dried winter melon strips
5 ml (1 teaspoon) salt
250 g (8 oz) edible chrysanthemum leaves or spinach
300 ml (½ pint) *dashi*
45 ml (3 tablespoons) caster sugar
25 ml (1½ tablespoons) soy sauce
15 ml (1 tablespoon) *mirin*

Pour boiling water over the *aburage* to remove any residual oiliness, then cut each cake in half to make 4 squares. Gently pull the outside skins apart to open up each square into a pocket. Take care not to tear the outside skin. Wash the winter melon strips, then rub with the salt between the hands. Rinse well and put into a pan of clean water to boil for 10 minutes. Drain and leave until required. (If using Chinese dried winter melon see page 173 for method of preparation.) Wash the chrysanthemum leaves and boil fast in lightly salted water for 4 minutes. Cool quickly under the cold tap and drain well. Cut the chrysanthemum stalks into 4-cm (1½-inch) lengths. Bring the *dashi* to the boil and lift from the heat. Break an egg into each pouch, then carefully close the open end and tie securely with a strip of winter melon. As each pouch is prepared drop it into the hot *dashi*. When all the pouches are filled return the pan to the heat and season the *dashi* with 10 ml (2 teaspoons) sugar and 15 ml (1 tablespoon) soy sauce. Simmer for 10 minutes, then add the remaining sugar, soy sauce and *mirin*. Continue simmering for another 10 minutes. Remove from the heat, but leave the pouches in the simmering sauce until ready to serve. Serve with the chrysanthemum leaves and spoon over a little of the simmering sauce.

If using spinach, de-vein the spinach leaves, wash and boil in salted water for 5 minutes. Then refresh under the cold tap, drain and cut into 4-cm (1½-inch) lengths.

Salads

Almost every Japanese main meal includes at least one salad of lightly cooked vegetables or fresh vegetables with a dressing. These dressings range from simple sweet and sour (sugar and vinegar) through various nut pastes and egg-thickened sauces to beancurd creams and *miso*-flavoured dressings, and can be used in almost limitless combinations with a wide choice of vegetables.

For convenience the recipes in this chapter have been divided into 'simple salads', made only with vegetables (the kind of salad most often eaten at family meals), and 'mixed salads', made with more expensive ingredients such as crab or chicken mixed with an assortment of vegetables. The mixed salads are suitable for more formal meals.

Some of the 'simple' salads can be used together as part of an *hors d'oeuvre* of various vegetables, fish and seafoods served at the beginning of a big formal meal. Other recipes in the same section are a part of the series of vinegared-vegetable dishes that range from small appetizers eaten with *sake* through to the pickles eaten as a relish with rice as part of the most basic Japanese meal (*miso* soup, pickles and rice). Yet other recipes, still consisting only of vegetables but with more elaborate dressings, are sometimes served as small side dishes in a large-scale dinner.

Also included in this chapter is a section of recipes called 'appetizers'. These are not strictly salads but small savoury dishes served with *sake*, and represent a few of the many snacks sold in Japan's ubiquitous small bars. In these, drinkers may order such dishes as grilled chicken kebabs, octopus tentacles in vinegar, dishes of boiled cow-peas – similar to broad beans – or other vinegared salads such as carrot and white radish, or squid and cucumber, to eat with their *sake* or beer.

Simple salads

Asparagus in egg sauce

Serves 4

350-g (12-oz) can of asparagus or
 20 stalks of fresh asparagus

Dressing:
1 egg yolk
15 ml (1 tablespoon) soy sauce

Drain and dip the asparagus in hot water to heat through. (If using fresh asparagus cook gently in boiling water until just tender.) Cut into 5-cm (2-inch) lengths. Beat the egg yolk with the soy sauce and pour over the asparagus. Serve hot in small individual dishes.

Asparagus with sesame seeds

Serves 4

The Japanese use a ceramic pestle and mortar for all grinding jobs. It is not smooth-sided like the Western version but made with corrugated fine ridges running down from the rim to the base. It is an extremely efficient food grinder. A food processor can be used, just as efficiently, but for grinding small quantities of food such as sesame seeds the best results are obtained using a rolling-pin on a large flat surface – a pastry board, for example.

350-g (12-oz) can of asparagus or
 20 stalks of fresh asparagus

Dressing:
30 ml (2 tablespoons) white sesame seeds
25 ml (1½ tablespoons) *dashi*
15 ml (1 tablespoon) soy sauce

Drain the canned asparagus and cut into 7-cm (3-inch) lengths. (If using fresh asparagus, trim to leave only the soft green heads and boil gently in salted water for 5 minutes. Rinse immediately in cold water and drain well.) Toast the sesame seeds in a dry pan over a moderate heat until golden brown. Shake or stir continually to prevent burning.

Crush the seeds either with a pestle and mortar or with a rolling-pin on a board. Mix the sesame with the *dashi* and soy sauce, then mix into the asparagus. Serve in small individual bowls.

Lightly cooked french beans, cut into 5-cm (2-inch) lengths, can be served with the same dressing.

Aubergines with a sesame dressing

Serves 4

200 g (7 oz) aubergines
5 ml (1 teaspoon) salt

Dressing:
25 ml (1½ tablespoons) sesame seeds
25 ml (1½ tablespoons) *dashi*
25 ml (1½ tablespoons) soy sauce
25 ml (1½ tablespoons) rice vinegar
10 ml (2 teaspoons) caster sugar

Cut the aubergines into slices 3 mm (1/10-inch) thick, then cut each slice into strips about ½ cm (¼ inch) wide. Soak in cold water for 30 minutes to remove any bitterness. Toast the sesame seeds in a dry pan over a moderate heat until golden brown. Shake or stir continually to prevent burning, then crush either in a pestle and mortar or with a rolling-pin on a board until about half the seeds are broken. Mix with the other ingredients of the dressing. Put the aubergines into 1 litre (2 pints) boiling water with 5 ml (1 teaspoon) salt. Boil until soft (about 5 minutes), then drain well. Arrange a small pile of aubergine strips in the centre of each serving bowl and spoon over the seasoning sauce. Serve cold.

French bean salad

Serves 4

180 g (6 oz) french beans

Dressing:
25 ml (1½ tablespoons) soy sauce
10 ml (2 teaspoons) *sake*
5 ml (1 teaspoon) *mirin*
1.5 ml (¼ teaspoon) salt
1.5 ml (¼ teaspoon) ginger juice

2.5 ml (½ teaspoon) sesame seeds

Top and tail the beans, and string if necessary. Boil in lightly salted water for 5 minutes, then rinse in cold water and drain well. Mix the dressing. Toast the sesame seeds in a dry pan over a moderate heat until golden brown. Shake or stir continually to prevent burning. Toss the beans in the dressing and divide between four small plates. Sprinkle with toasted sesame seeds.

French beans with beancurd dressing

Serves 4

180 g (6 oz) french beans or frozen sliced beans

Dressing:
150 g (5 oz) beancurd
45 ml (3 tablespoons) sesame seeds*
25 ml (1½ tablespoons) white *miso*
10 ml (2 teaspoons) *mirin*
sugar and salt to taste

Top and tail the beans, then par-boil in lightly salted water for 5 minutes. Refresh in cold water, drain and cut into thin diagonal slices. If using frozen sliced beans, boil in salted water for 1 minute, then drain well. Dip the beancurd in boiling water for 30 seconds, drain for a few moments, then mash in a bowl with a fork. Toast the sesame seeds in a dry pan over a moderate heat until golden brown. Shake or stir continually to prevent burning. Crush the toasted sesame seeds either in a pestle and mortar or with a rolling-pin on a board until they make a smooth paste, then stir into the beancurd with the *miso* and *mirin*. Season to taste with sugar and salt and mix with the beans. Serve in small individual bowls.

An alternative salad using the same dressing can be made with 75 g (3 oz) beans and 75 g (3 oz) par-boiled carrot matchsticks.

Beansprouts with aburage in a mustard and vinegar dressing

Serves 4–8

This can be served either as a salad within a meal (4 servings) or as an appetizer to accompany *sake* (8 servings).

300 g (10 oz) beansprouts
5 ml (1 teaspoon) rice vinegar
1 cake of *aburage* (see page 106)

Dressing:
30 ml (2 tablespoons) rice vinegar
15 ml (1 tablespoon) caster sugar
2.5 ml (½ teaspoon) salt
3.5 ml (¾ teaspoon) made English mustard

Trim the roots from the beansprouts and rinse. Blanch in boiling water for 1 minute and drain well. Sprinkle the vinegar over. Pour boiling water over the *aburage* to remove any oiliness and cut into thin strips. Just before serving make the dressing and mix with the beansprouts and *aburage*.

---

* Chinese sesame paste or *tahina* may be substituted, but the flavour is not as good.

Beansprouts with pickled plums

Serves 4

250 g (8 oz) beansprouts
25 g (1 oz) cress
pinch of salt
1 pickled plum (see page 167)
15 ml (1 tablespoon) soy sauce
7.5 ml (1½ teaspoons) *mirin*

Trim the roots from the beansprouts and blanch in boiling water for 1 minute. Then drain well. Cut the roots from the cress, rinse and drain well. Mix the beansprouts and cress together with the salt. Remove the stone from the pickled plum and mash the flesh. Mix with the soy sauce and *mirin* and toss the beansprouts and cress in this dressing. Serve on individual small plates.

Broccoli with sesame seeds

Serves 4

250 g (8 oz) broccoli (calabrese)

Dressing:
30 ml (2 tablespoons) sesame seeds
25 ml (1½ tablespoons) *dashi*
15 ml (1 tablespoon) soy sauce

Pare the skin from the thick central stalk of the broccoli, then cut both the head and stalk into small pieces. Boil in lightly salted water for 4 minutes and refresh in cold water. Drain well. Toast the sesame seeds in a dry pan over a moderate heat until golden brown. Shake or stir continually to prevent burning. Crush with either a pestle and mortar or with a rolling-pin on a board. Stir the crushed sesame seeds into the *dashi* and soy sauce. Mix the dressing with the broccoli and serve in small individual dishes.

Broccoli with a mustard dressing

Serves 4

250 g (8 oz) broccoli (calabrese or purple sprouting)

Dressing:
30 ml (2 tablespoons) rice vinegar
10 ml (2 teaspoons) caster sugar
15 ml (1 tablespoon) soy sauce
2.5 ml (½ teaspoon) made English mustard

Trim and cut the broccoli into small florets. If using calabrese, pare the skin from the thick central stalk and cut it into batons about 5 cm (2 inches) long and 1 cm (½ inch) square. Boil the broccoli in lightly salted water for 4 minutes. Then immediately plunge into cold water and afterwards drain well. Just before serving mix the dressing and sprinkle it over the broccoli. Serve in small individual dishes.

Broccoli with an egg and vinegar dressing

Serves 4

250 g (8 oz) broccoli
30 ml (2 tablespoons) rice vinegar
1.5 ml (¼ teaspoon) salt
2 sticks of celery

Dressing:
1 egg yolk
15 ml (1 tablespoon) *mirin*
15 ml (1 tablespoon) *dashi*
45 ml (3 tablespoons) rice vinegar
1.5 ml (¼ teaspoon) salt

Trim and cut the broccoli into small florets. If using calabrese, pare the skin from the thick central stalk and cut it into batons, 1 cm (½ inch) wide and 5 cm (2 inches) long. Boil in lightly salted water for 4 minutes, then immediately cool in cold water. Drain well. Mix with the vinegar and salt and leave to marinate. Wash, trim and cut the celery into thin shreds, about 5 cm (2 inches) long. Add to the broccoli in the marinade. Mix the dressing in a double boiler and cook, stirring all the time, over gently boiling water until the mixture thickens (about 10 minutes). Leave to cool. Then drain the broccoli and celery and arrange on small individual dishes. Spoon over the dressing and serve.

Carrot and konnyaku salad with a beancurd dressing

Serves 4

In Japan dressings made with beancurd are called 'white dressing', and are very popular. The ingredients vary, sometimes including white *miso* or soy sauce together with a little vinegar and *mirin*. Various vegetables may be dressed in this way, including par-boiled sweet potatoes, white radish, green beans or dried mushrooms.

100 g (4 oz) carrot
100 g (4 oz) *konnyaku*

Simmering stock for vegetables:
200 ml (⅓ pint) *dashi*
15 ml (1 tablespoon) soy sauce
10 ml (2 teaspoons) caster sugar
30 ml (2 tablespoons) *sake*

Dressing:
150 g (5 oz) beancurd
45 ml (3 tablespoons) sesame seeds*
30 ml (2 tablespoons) sugar
1.5 ml (¼ teaspoon) salt

Peel and cut the carrot into thin strips about 1 cm (½ inch) wide and 5 cm (2 inches) long. Boil in lightly salted water for 2 minutes, then refresh under cold water. Drain well. Cut the *konnyaku* into slices the

* Chinese sesame paste or *tahina* may be substituted but are less satisfactory.

same size as the carrot and put into boiling water. Boil for 2 minutes, then transfer to a dry pan and dry over a moderate heat for 1–2 minutes. Bring the simmering stock to the boil in a small saucepan and add the carrot and *konnyaku*. Simmer for 4 minutes, then leave to cool in the stock.

Dip the beancurd in boiling water for 30 seconds, then lift out and mash in a bowl. Toast the sesame seeds in a dry frying-pan over a moderate heat until golden brown. Stir or shake to prevent burning. Then grind with a pestle and mortar or crush to a paste with a rolling-pin on a board. Mix the sesame paste into the beancurd and add sugar and salt to taste. The mixture should have a creamy consistency like thick mayonnaise. Just before serving mix with the drained carrot and *konnyaku*.

Carrot and white radish salad

Serves 4

Serve this salad as a small dish with a meal or in very small quantities as an appetizer to accompany *sake*. It is better made well in advance and served thoroughly chilled.

75 g (3 oz) carrot
225 g (9 oz) white radish
2.5 ml (½ teaspoon) salt

Dressing:
45 ml (3 tablespoons) rice vinegar
2.5 ml (½ teaspoon) soy sauce
10 ml (2 teaspoons) caster sugar

Peel and cut the carrot and white radish into matchsticks about 5 cm (2 inches) long. Sprinkle with salt and leave to soften for 30 minutes. Then squeeze between the hands to get rid of all the excess water. Mix with the dressing and chill in the refrigerator for at least 8 hours. Serve in small individual bowls.

Chrysanthemum and nori rolls

Serves 4

500 g (1 lb) edible chrysanthemum leaves (see page 172) or 400 g (12 oz) spinach
7.5 ml (1½ teaspoons) soy sauce
4 sheets of *nori*

Dressing:
20 ml (4 teaspoons) soy sauce
7.5 ml (1½ teaspoons) lemon juice

Tear the leaves from the chrysanthemum stalks, discarding any tough leaves. Wash well and boil fast in lightly salted water for 4 minutes. Afterwards drain well and rinse immediately in cold water until cool. If using spinach, tear out the central vein and cook in the same manner. Squeeze out as much water as possible, and sprinkle with the soy sauce.

Toast the shiny side of each sheet of *nori* over a high heat from a gas or electric ring for about 3 seconds until it has changed from purple to green. Then cut each sheet in half. Lay one sheet of the *nori* across a rolling mat (see page 74) and spread a quarter of the chrysanthemum leaves over it. Then roll up the *nori* with the chrysanthemum leaves inside using the rolling mat to make a tight cylinder about 3 cm (1 inch) in diameter. Cut the roll into 5 equal slices and arrange in the shape of a flower on a small plate. Repeat with the remaining sheets of *nori*. Serve the dressing in tiny individual bowls as a dipping sauce.

Cucumber and wakame salad

Serves 4

150 g (5 oz) cucumber
10 ml (2 teaspoons) salt
25 g (1 oz) salted *wakame* or 10 g (½ oz) dried *wakame*

Dressing:
30 ml (2 tablespoons) rice vinegar
15 ml (1 tablespoon) water
15 ml (1 tablespoon) caster sugar
1.5 ml (¼ teaspoon) salt

Rub the cucumber in 5 ml (1 teaspoon) salt on a board, then rinse well. Cut into paper-thin slices and mix with the rest of the salt. Squeeze between the hands until the cucumber becomes soft and water runs out. Then rinse well and leave to drain. Wash the *wakame* and soak for 5 minutes in cold water. When soft, scald with boiling water then immediately rinse in cold water. Drain well, discard the hard edge and cut diagonally into 4-cm (1½-inch) lengths. Just before serving squeeze both the cucumber and *wakame* dry and mix with the dressing. Serve in individual small bowls. If using dried *wakame*, it is easier to cut it before scalding with boiling water.

Cucumber salad with miso dressing

Serves 4

150 g (5 oz) cucumber
10 ml (2 teaspoons) salt

Dressing:
7.5 ml (1½ teaspoons) red *miso*
2.5 ml (½ teaspoon) *mirin*

Rub the cucumber in 5 ml (1 teaspoon) salt on a board, then rinse well and cut into paper-thin slices. Mix with the rest of the salt and knead until soft. Squeeze out all the water, rinse well and drain. Mix the dressing to a smooth paste: if the *miso* is very stiff, add a little water or *dashi*. Just before serving squeeze the cucumber again and mix with the dressing.

Green salad with peanut dressing

Serves 4

The green vegetable used in this recipe is a variety of *Brassica chinensis* with green stalks, small green leaves and bright yellow flowers. It is one of the best southern Chinese winter greens and is grown in Japan during the summer. It is sold in many Chinese grocers in the UK under its Cantonese name *choisam*. Use cooked french beans or spinach as an alternative.

250 g (8 oz) *choisam*
5 ml (1 teaspoon) soy sauce

Dressing:
30 ml (2 tablespoons) peanut butter
15 ml (1 tablespoon) caster sugar
10 ml (2 teaspoons) soy sauce

Wash and trim the *choisam* and tie into bundles. Drop the bundles into boiling water and cook for 2 minutes. Then lift out and refresh immediately in cold water. Squeeze dry with the hands, cut free of the bundles and sprinkle with soy sauce. Squeeze again and cut the stalks into 3-cm (1-inch) lengths. Mix with the dressing and serve in small individual dishes.

Okra salad

Serves 4

20 okra pods
15 ml (1 tablespoon) *hanakatsuo* (see page 165)
15 ml (1 tablespoon) soy sauce

Scrape the okra lightly to remove the bloom from the skins, then wash very well. Do not cut off the stalk ends. Boil in lightly salted water for about 5 minutes, then refresh in cold water. Leave to drain. Just before serving, discard the stalk ends and cut the pods obliquely into 1-cm (½-inch) lengths. Divide into separate dishes and serve sprinkled with *hanakatsuo* and soy sauce.

Okra with natto

Serves 4

Natto, fermented soya beans, has a slightly putrid taste, and people either like it or loathe it. In Japan it is particularly popular in Tokyo and the north, where it is often served with rice at breakfast.

20 okra pods
1 packet of *natto*
10 ml (2 teaspoons) soy sauce

Scrape the okra lightly to remove the bloom from the skins and wash very well. Do not cut the pods. Place in slightly salted boiling water, boil for 5 minutes, then refresh in cold water. Drain well, cut off the stalk ends and slice the pods very finely. Mix with the *natto* and serve in small dishes with a little soy sauce poured over them.

Mixed salad with a miso dressing

Serves 4

50 g (2 oz) cucumber
2.5 ml (½ teaspoon) salt
2 small tomatoes
100 g (4 oz) lettuce leaves
25 g (1 oz) salted *wakame* or 10 g (½ oz) dried *wakame*

Dressing:
15 ml (1 tablespoon) white *miso*
15 ml (1 tablespoon) rice vinegar
7.5 ml (1½ teaspoons) caster sugar
1.5 ml (¼ teaspoon) made English mustard

Rub the cucumber in the salt on a board, then rinse well. Cut into thin oval slices. Cut the tomatoes into eighths. Wash, drain and shred the lettuce leaves coarsely. Wash and soak the *wakame* in cold water for 5 minutes, then scald with boiling water and immediately cool in cold water. Cut away the tough edge and slice into 4-cm (1½-inch) lengths. Arrange the vegetables in individual bowls and spoon over the dressing just before serving.

If using dried *wakame* it is easier to cut it before scalding with boiling water.

Sweet potatoes with a sour cucumber sauce

Serves 4

200 g (7 oz) sweet potatoes
oil for deep frying

Dressing:
75 g (3 oz) cucumber
45 ml (3 tablespoons) rice vinegar
15 ml (1 tablespoon) caster sugar
1.5 ml (¼ teaspoon) salt

Peel and cut the potatoes into dice, 1 cm (½ inch) square. Soak in cold water for 30 minutes, then drain and pat dry. Heat the deep fat and fry the potato dice for about 5–7 minutes, until just soft. Lift out and leave to drain. Grate the cucumber and leave to drain. Just before serving squeeze out the cucumber and mix it with the rest of the dressing. Arrange the potato dice in individual bowls and spoon over the cucumber sauce.

Spinach with beancurd dressing

Serves 4

Japanese spinach is usually a form of Swiss chard or leaf beet. The leaves have thin stems which join together at the top of the root. The leaves are not cut individually, but very young whole plants are gathered and sold with the root still attached. In the UK this type of spinach beet is sometimes sold in West Indian markets (called *pallack* spinach) or in Chinese or Indian grocers, but the quality always seems poor.

In Japan the spinach is washed and cooked in boiling salted water before the root is cut from the leaves. When using young leaf beet it is not necessary to tear out the central veins.

300 g (10 oz) fresh spinach, or frozen leaf spinach
5 ml (1 teaspoon) soy sauce

———

Dressing:
150 g (5 oz) beancurd
45 ml (3 tablespoons) sesame seeds*
2.5 ml (½ teaspoon) salt, or more (to taste)
20 ml (4 teaspoons) caster sugar, or to taste

Wash the spinach and discard any badly damaged leaves. Tear out the tough central vein. Put into boiling salted water for 2–3 minutes and afterwards refresh immediately in cold water. Squeeze firmly between the hands until dry, then sprinkle with the soy sauce and squeeze again. Cut into roughly 3-cm (1-inch) lengths.

To make the dressing, dip the beancurd into boiling water for 30 seconds. Drain for a few seconds, then mash in a bowl. Toast the sesame seeds in a dry pan over a moderate heat until golden brown. Shake or stir continually to prevent burning. Grind very finely until oily, either with a pestle and mortar or with a rolling-pin on a board (better still an electric grinder, e.g. a coffee mill). Beat the paste into the beancurd and add the sugar and salt to taste. The dressing should be smooth and creamy. Mix with the spinach and serve in individual small bowls.

* Chinese sesame paste or *tahina* may be used instead of sesame seeds, but the flavour is not as good.

Spinach with hanakatsuo

Serves 4

This recipe is very typical of the simple vegetarian dishes so often included in a Japanese family meal. Neither this nor the following recipe would be suitable for a more formal meal.

300 g (10 oz) fresh spinach
5 ml (1 teaspoon) soy sauce
30 ml (2 tablespoons) *hanakatsuo* or 60 ml (4 tablespoons) finely shredded *nori*

Wash the spinach and discard any badly damaged leaves. Tear out the tough central vein. Boil in lightly salted water for 2–3 minutes, then refresh immediately in cold water. Squeeze the spinach between the hands until quite dry, then sprinkle the soy sauce over. Squeeze again. Make sure that the soy sauce is well distributed through all the spinach. Squeeze into a firm dry roll, then cut into 4-cm (1½-inch) lengths and arrange a portion on each serving dish. Scatter *hanakatsuo* over the top of each helping or if preferred 15 ml (1 tablespoon) finely shredded *nori*.

Spinach with a sesame dressing

Serves 4

300 g (10 oz) fresh spinach or frozen leaf spinach
5 ml (1 teaspoon) soy sauce

Dressing:
45 ml (3 tablespoons) sesame seeds
25 ml (1½ tablespoons) soy sauce
15 ml (1 tablespoon) caster sugar
15 ml (1 tablespoon) *dashi*

Wash the spinach and tear out the tough central veins. Boil in salted water for 2–3 minutes, then refresh immediately in cold water. (If using frozen spinach, dip in boiling salted water for 1 minute, then cool quickly under the cold tap.) Squeeze the spinach between the hands to dry, then sprinkle with 5 ml (1 teaspoon) soy sauce. Squeeze dry again and cut into 3-cm (1-inch) lengths.

Toast the sesame seeds in a dry pan over a moderate heat until golden brown. Shake or stir continually to prevent burning. Crush in a pestle and mortar or with a rolling-pin on a board until about half of the seeds are broken. Mix with the soy sauce, sugar and *dashi*, then lightly stir into the spinach. Serve in individual small bowls.

Vinegared turnips

500 g (1 lb) young turnips
20 ml (4 teaspoons) salt

Dressing:
150 g (5 oz) rice vinegar
75 ml (5 tablespoons) caster sugar
2.5 ml (½ teaspoon) soy sauce

---

2 dried chillis or 3-cm (1-inch) square *yuzu* peel (or lemon peel) and 3-cm (1-inch) square *konbu*

Peel and remove the tops from the turnips. Turn upside-down and stand between two chopsticks on a chopping-board. Using a thin, sharp knife slice across the turnip at 2-mm ($\frac{1}{12}$-inch) intervals down to the chopsticks, which act as guards ensuring that the slices remain joined at the bottom. Then turn the turnip between the chopsticks and repeat the slicing at right angles to the previous cuts. Use the same 'chrysanthemum cut' on the rest of the turnips. Soak the cut turnips with 20 ml (4 teaspoons) salt in 300 ml (½ pint) cold water for 30 minutes. Then squeeze dry and cut into quarters or eighths, depending on size. Put into a clean bowl and pour over the dressing. De-seed and finely chop the chillis, or finely slice the *yuzu* and *konbu* and add to the turnips. Stir carefully to ensure the turnip is well coated with the vinegar and sugar and cover the bowl with cling-wrap. Leave in the refrigerator for at least 5 days before eating. Every 2–3 days mix with a clean spoon to make sure the turnip remains soaking in the marinade. These turnips will keep for 3 weeks.

Mixed salads

Chicken and tomato salad

Serves 4

250 g (8 oz) chicken leg

Marinade:
1.5 ml (¼ teaspoon) salt
5 ml (1 teaspoon) *sake*

---

200 g (7 oz) cucumber
5 ml (1 teaspoon) salt
150 g (5 oz) tomatoes

Dressing:
30 ml (2 tablespoons) rice vinegar
2.5 ml (½ teaspoon) salt
5 ml (1 teaspoon) caster sugar
10 ml (2 teaspoons) *mirin*
30 ml (2 tablespoons) *dashi*
2.5 ml (½ teaspoon) *kudzu* flour (see page 170) or arrowroot

Marinate the chicken for 15 minutes, then steam with the marinade in a bowl over a high heat for 20 minutes. Leave to cool, then remove the bones and cut the meat into small pieces. Wash the cucumber and cut in half lengthways. Stand one half, cut-side-down, between two chopsticks and make a series of deep cuts at 1-mm ($\frac{1}{20}$-inch) intervals along its length. Then cut in half lengthways and cut each piece into 2-cm (1-inch) lengths. Repeat with the other half cucumber and sprinkle 5 ml (1 teaspoon) salt over all the pieces. Leave to drain. Skin and de-seed the tomatoes and cut the flesh into 1-cm (½-inch) squares. Mix the dressing ingredients in a small pan and stir over a moderate heat until it boils and thickens. Leave on one side to cool. Carefully arrange the chicken, tomato and cucumber on four separate plates, and spoon over a portion of dressing before serving.

Chicken and lettuce rolls

Serves 4

200 g (7 oz) chicken breast

Marinade:
15 ml (1 tablespoon) rice vinegar
15 ml (1 tablespoon) soy sauce
15 ml (1 tablespoon) black fungus
5 large lettuce leaves

Dressing:
15 ml (1 tablespoon) white *miso*
6.5 ml (1¼ teaspoons) caster sugar
1.5 ml (¼ teaspoon) made English mustard
15 ml (1 tablespoon) rice vinegar

Make numerous slashes along the chicken breast and drop into lightly salted boiling water. Boil for 5 minutes, or until just cooked through, then plunge immediately into iced water to cool quickly. Pat dry and marinate for 30 minutes. Soak the black fungus in hand-hot water for 30 minutes, then rinse well and discard any hard pieces. Cut into thin strips. Wash and dry the lettuce leaves and tear off the bottom of the main stalks. Cut the chicken lengthwise into five equal strips. Spread out a lettuce leaf and lay a strip of chicken and a few shreds of black fungus along its main vein. Roll up the lettuce leaf as tightly as possible around the chicken. Cut the roll into diagonal slices about 4 cm (1¼ inches) wide, discarding any extra bits of leaf. Repeat with the other leaves and remaining chicken. Mix the dressing. Arrange a few slices of chicken roll on each small plate and spoon over the dressing before serving.

Chicken and mushroom salad with a walnut dressing

Serves 4

150 g (5 oz) boned chicken breast
pinch of salt
15 ml (1 tablespoon) *sake*
150 g (5 oz) french beans
5 ml (1 teaspoon) salt
15 ml (1 tablespoon) rice vinegar
4 large fresh mushrooms

Dressing:
50 g (2 oz) shelled walnuts
45 ml (3 tablespoons) rice vinegar
30 ml (2 tablespoons) caster sugar
2.5 ml (½ teaspoon) salt
5 ml (1 teaspoon) soy sauce

Sprinkle the chicken breast with the salt and *sake* and steam it in a bowl over a high heat for 20 minutes. Remove from the heat and allow to cool in the cooking liquor. When the chicken is cold enough to handle, cut into matchsticks. Meanwhile top and tail french beans and rub in 5 ml (1 teaspoon) salt on a board. Then drop into boiling water and boil for 5 minutes. Drain and refresh with cold water. Finally, cut diagonally into 3-cm (1-inch) lengths and sprinkle with 15 ml (1 tablespoon) rice vinegar. Leave on one side to marinate. Wipe the mushroom caps. Cut off the stalks and discard. Put the caps under a hot grill for about 4 minutes, turning once. Then slice very finely.

Soak the walnuts in boiling water and peel off their skins: this is a very fiddly job and takes a long time, but the final result is a much smoother dressing. Grind or crush the peeled walnuts as finely as possible using either a pestle and mortar or a rolling-pin on a board. Afterwards mix into the rest of the dressing and beat hard until smooth and creamy (a liquidizer helps at this stage). Fold the chicken, drained beans and mushrooms into the dressing and serve on small individual plates.

Chicken and wakame seaweed with miso dressing

Serves 4

100 g (4 oz) boned chicken breast
pinch of salt
5 ml (1 teaspoon) *sake*
20 g (¾ oz) salted *wakame* or
 1 length dried *wakame*
75 g (3 oz) cucumber
5 ml (1 teaspoon) salt

Dressing:
15 ml (1 tablespoon) red *miso*
12.5 ml (2½ teaspoons) caster sugar
15 ml (1 tablespoon) rice vinegar

Put the chicken breast in a small bowl with the salt and *sake* into a steamer over a high heat. Steam for 20 minutes. Remove from the heat and allow to cool in the cooking liquor. Meanwhile soak the *wakame* in cold water for 5 minutes. Drain and scald with boiling water. Rinse immediately in cold water. Trim off the thick edge and roughly cut the soft leaves into 5-cm (2-inch) lengths. Unless the cucumber is very thin, cut it in half lengthways, and slice each half very finely. Sprinkle with 5 ml (1 teaspoon) salt and squeeze between the fingers until the water runs out and the cucumber becomes quite soft. Rinse well in cold water and squeeze dry again. Leave to drain. When the chicken is cold, cut the meat and skin into thin strips. Mix the dressing. Just before serving mix the chicken, cucumber and *wakame* into the dressing and divide between four small bowls.

Chicken and white radish salad

Serves 4

150 g (5 oz) boned chicken breast
1.5 ml (¼ teaspoon) salt
5 ml (1 teaspoon) *sake*
2 dried mushrooms
5 ml (1 teaspoon) soy sauce
25 g (1 oz) french beans
1 stick of celery
75 g (3 oz) white radish

Dressing:
25 ml (1½ tablespoons) caster sugar
2.5 ml (½ teaspoon) salt
15 ml (1 tablespoon) soy sauce
40 ml (2½ tablespoons) rice vinegar

Sprinkle the chicken breast with the salt and *sake*. Put in a bowl, then put the bowl in a steamer and steam over a high heat for 20 minutes. Then remove from the heat and allow to cool in the cooking liquor. When it is cold enough to handle, cut into matchsticks. Soak the mushrooms in warm water for 30 minutes, then, reserving the soaking water, remove the hard stalks. Put the caps with 60 ml (4 tablespoons) of the reserved soaking water and 5 ml (1 teaspoon) soy sauce into a small pan and simmer until quite soft and almost dry. Afterwards cut the caps into thin strips. Top and tail the french beans and boil in lightly salted water for 5 minutes. Then refresh in cold water and cut into 3-cm (1-inch) lengths. Wash and cut the celery into matchsticks about 4 cm (1½ inches) long. Peel and shred the white radish. Mix the dressing and pour over the chicken. Leave to marinate for 5 minutes before adding the mushrooms, beans, celery and white radish. Mix well and serve in four small bowls.

Crab and cauliflower with a vinegar and egg sauce

Serves 4

150 g (5 oz) cauliflower

Marinade:
60 ml (4 tablespoons) rice vinegar
2.5 ml (½ teaspoon) salt
50 g (2 oz) french beans or mange-tout peas
1 medium-sized crab or 100 g (4 oz) white crab meat

Dressing:
1 egg yolk
45 ml (3 tablespoons) rice vinegar
30 ml (2 tablespoons) *dashi*
15 ml (1 tablespoon) *mirin*
1.5 ml (¼ teaspoon) salt
5 ml (1 teaspoon) sugar

Wash and cut the cauliflower into florets and cook for 5 minutes in lightly salted boiling water. Then drain well and put into the marinade. Trim the beans (or peas) and cook in lightly salted water for 7 minutes. Refresh immediately under cold water and cut diagonally into 5-cm (2-inch) lengths. Put to marinate with the cauliflower. Remove all the meat from the crab (see below for instructions) and mix with 5 ml (1 teaspoon) of the marinating vinegar.

Beat all the ingredients for the dressing together and cook in a double boiler until the mixture thickens. Do not use too high a heat or the egg will curdle. When the mixture is thick and creamy remove from the heat and leave to cool. Just before serving, drain the cauliflower and beans and arrange in individual bowls. Add a portion of crab meat to each and spoon over the dressing.

To dress a boiled crab Remove the claws and separate the carapace, or big shell, from the body. Remove the stomach sac from just behind the mouth in the carapace, and the greyish feathery gills which surround the body. Once these are removed everything else in the crab is edible. Scrape out the soft brown meat from the inside of the carapace and pick off the white meat from around the hard body. Crack the claws and pick out the meat. Use as directed.

Ham salad

Serves 4

75 g (3 oz) cucumber
5 ml (1 teaspoon) salt
50 g (2 oz) carrot
75 g (3 oz) white radish
50 g (2 oz) cooked lean ham
30 ml (2 tablespoons) sesame seeds

Dressing:
30 ml (2 tablespoons) *dashi*
30 ml (2 tablespoons) rice vinegar
7.5 ml (1½ teaspoons) soy sauce
5 ml (1 teaspoon) caster sugar
pinch of salt

Roll the cucumber in the salt on a board, then leave for 30 minutes. Afterwards rinse and cut into matchsticks. Peel and cut the carrot and white radish into similar-sized sticks. Soak in lightly salted water for 20 minutes, then drain well and gently squeeze between the hands. Cut the ham into matchsticks. Toast the sesame seeds in a dry pan over a moderate heat until golden brown. Shake or stir the pan continually to prevent burning. Turn out and leave to cool. Mix the dressing, pour over the vegetables and ham and mix well. Serve in tidy mounds on individual plates and scatter over the toasted sesame seeds.

Prawn and mushroom salad with a beancurd and sesame dressing

Serves 4

5 small dried mushrooms
7.5 ml (1½ teaspoons) caster sugar
10 ml (2 teaspoons) soy sauce
8 raw prawns*
5 ml (1 teaspoon) rice vinegar
150 g (5 oz) cucumber
2.5 ml (½ teaspoon) salt

Dressing:
150 g (5 oz) beancurd
45 ml (3 tablespoons) sesame seeds†
45 ml (3 tablespoons) rice vinegar
4 ml (¾ teaspoon) salt
40 ml (2½ tablespoons) caster sugar

---

5 g (¼ oz) ginger

Soak the mushrooms in warm water for 30 minutes, then, reserving the soaking water, discard the hard stalks and cut the caps into thin slices. Mix 45 ml (3 tablespoons) of the reserved soaking water with 5 ml (1 teaspoon) of sugar and the soy sauce in a small pan and simmer the mushroom slices for 5 minutes, taking care they do not boil dry. Drain and leave to cool. Shell and de-vein the prawns and boil in lightly salted water for 2 minutes. Then drain and marinate with 2.5 ml (½ teaspoon) sugar and the vinegar for 30 minutes. Meanwhile wash the cucumber and cut into very fine slices. Sprinkle with the salt and knead with the hands until it becomes soft and starts to run with water. Then squeeze well and leave to drain.

Drop the beancurd into boiling water for 30 seconds, then lift out and mash in a bowl with a spoon. Toast the sesame seeds in a dry pan over a moderate heat until golden brown. Shake or stir continually to prevent burning. Crush to a smooth, oily paste either using a pestle and mortar or with a rolling-pin on a board. Beat this paste into the mashed beancurd and stir in the salt, vinegar and sugar to make a thick, smooth cream. Peel the ginger and cut into very fine, hair-like threads. Just before serving mix the mushrooms, prawns and cucumber into the dressing and divide between four small bowls. Scatter the finely shredded ginger over.

* Raw prawns in the UK are grey, frozen, uncooked prawns.
† Chinese sesame paste or *tahina* may be substituted but are less satisfactory.

Squid and cucumber salad with a ginger dressing

Serves 4

350 g (12 oz) squid
150 g (5 oz) cucumber

——

Dressing:
45 ml (3 tablespoons) rice vinegar
25 ml (1½ tablespoons) soy sauce
15 ml (1 tablespoon) *mirin*
15 ml (1 tablespoon) *dashi*
1.5 ml (¼ teaspoon) sesame oil
15 ml (1 tablespoon) caster sugar

——

25 g (1 oz) ginger

Clean the squid as directed on page 55. Cut down the body to make a flat sheet, and on the *outside*, score all over it with a criss-cross pattern. Then, holding the knife at an acute angle to the squid, cut it into bite-sized pieces. Wash the cucumber and cut in half lengthways. Lay one-half between two chopsticks, which will act as guards, and make a series of cuts down to the chopsticks at 2-mm (1/12-inch) intervals along its length. Then cut the slashed cucumber in half lengthways, and cut both pieces into 2-cm (¾-inch) lengths. Repeat with the second half of the cucumber. Soak the cucumber pieces in cold water until required. Bring 600 ml (1 pint) salted water to the boil and drop in the squid pieces. Remove immediately the water returns to the boil and plunge into iced water. Drain well.

Mix the ingredients of the dressing in a small pan and heat until the sugar is dissolved. Leave on one side to cool. Grate 20 g (¾ oz) of the ginger and squeeze the juice into the dressing. Cut the remaining 5 g (¼ oz) into hair-like shreds. Just before serving drain the cucumber thoroughly and arrange with the squid in four small bowls. Pour over the dressing and garnish with the threads of ginger.

Appetizers

Grilled chicken and nori slices

Serves 4

1 egg
200 g (7 oz) chicken scraps
1 egg white
5 ml (1 teaspoon) caster sugar
2.5 ml (½ teaspoon) soy sauce
1 standard sheet *nori*, 20 × 15 cm (8 × 6 inches)

——

Grilling sauce:
45 ml (3 tablespoons) soy sauce
90 ml (6 tablespoons) *mirin*

Beat the egg and scramble over a moderate heat in a small pan without any oil until it just begins to break but is still damp. Mince the chicken scraps finely and mix with the lightly scrambled egg, egg white, sugar and soy sauce in a food processor or liquidizer until a smooth, sticky paste (the Japanese use a pestle and mortar). Hold the sheet of *nori*, shiny-side-down, over either a gas or an electric ring full on for about 3 seconds while it turns from purple to green. Then cut into 8 equal rectangles. Mix the grilling sauce in a small saucepan and bring to the boil over a moderate heat. Boil for about 3 minutes to reduce the sauce by one-third.

Spread a layer of the chicken paste about 1 cm (½ inch) thick over each sheet of *nori*. Smooth over the top with a wet knife, then brush with the grilling sauce. Under a hot grill cook the slices, chicken-side-up, for 3 minutes. Then turn over and brush the *nori* side with the sauce. Grill this way up for 2 minutes. Brush the *nori* a second time with the sauce and continue grilling, *nori*-side-up, for another 2 minutes. Finally, turn the slices again and brush the chicken side with the remaining sauce. Grill for another 2 minutes. Serve hot or cold.

Steamed chicken squares

Serves 4

40 g (1½ oz) carrot
5 small mushrooms
350 g (12 oz) minced chicken

———

Seasoning sauce:
70 ml (4½ tablespoons) soy sauce
45 ml (3 tablespoons) *mirin*
45 ml (3 tablespoons) caster sugar
5 ml (1 teaspoon) *miso*

———

1 egg white
4 egg yolks
2 french beans

Mince the carrot and mushrooms very finely and mix with half the minced chicken. Put the seasoning sauce into a small pan and add the chicken mixture and vegetables. Stir over a high heat until it boils, making sure all the chicken is well broken up, then turn down the heat and simmer until the mixture is almost dry. Lift off the heat and allow to cool. Mix the uncooked portions of chicken with the egg white, and when cold beat in the cooked chicken and vegetables. Line a 1-lb loaf-tin with oiled tinfoil, extending it over the sides at each end. Fill with the mixture and smooth the top. Cover with a cloth and steam over fast-boiling water for 20 minutes. Meanwhile, top and tail the french beans and cook in lightly salted water for 5 minutes. Drain and chop very finely. Mix with the well-beaten egg yolks. When the chicken is cooked wipe the moisture from the top and pour the beaten egg and beans over it. Return to the steamer and steam for another 2–3 minutes. Then remove from the steamer and leave to cool. When cold, lift the cake out of the loaf-tin, cut into twelve rectangles and serve.

Soups

Soup is a part of almost every meal in Japan, including breakfast. For most family meals, and always at breakfast, it is made with a seaweed-based stock (*dashi*) into which several spoonfuls of fermented soya-bean paste (*miso*) are stirred. The *miso* thickens the soup and gives it a savoury, appetizing flavour. *Miso* soups are always garnished with a seasonal selection of vegetables, beancurd or sometimes fish or meat.

In Japan *miso* soups have been a basic family dish for generations, eaten by peasants and townspeople alike. The daily use of *miso*, with its high protein amino-acid content, is said to be one reason why the Japanese peasants were able to survive and work on their meagre diet during the seventeenth and eighteenth centuries. Now, with increasing affluence and a greatly increased choice of protein foods, *miso* soup plays a less vital part in the Japanese diet.

Another standard soup is clear, and is served mainly at formal meals, although it may also be included in family meals. Like the *miso* soup it is based on *dashi* stock and is served with a wide variety of different garnishes, such as pieces of chicken, fish, seafood and vegetables. These are combined according to their seasonal availability, as are the garnishes for *miso* soup. There are no set rules and the ingredients can be varied and mixed at will. Part of the attraction of

Japanese clear soups is the pattern and contrasts of colour, shape and texture visible through the clear liquid. Both *miso* and clear soups are served in deep lacquer bowls, usually red or black, which are designed to retain the heat. These often have domed lids.

Dashi, the basic stock for all soups, remains to this day traditionally vegetarian and Buddhist. It is made from either *konbu* seaweed (kelp) alone, or from a combination of *konbu* and dried fish flakes. It is quick and easy to make and does not require the long, slow boiling needed for meat-based stocks in the West. Modern Japanese households, although they now freely use meat of all kinds, do not usually have bones or chicken carcasses available from which to make meat stocks. Instant *dashi* powder, as well as instant stock cubes, are frequently used by Japanese housewives for soups and other dishes.

Dashi with konbu and hanakatsuo

10 cm (4 inches) *konbu*
12 g ($\frac{1}{2}$ oz) *hanakatsuo*

Wipe the *konbu* and place in a saucepan with 1 litre ($1\frac{3}{4}$ pints) cold water over a low heat. Bring slowly towards boiling point, but when the bubbles at the bottom of the pan start to rise to the top lift out the *konbu* and discard. Raise the heat and as the water starts to boil throw in the *hanakatsuo*. Wait until the water foams up, then remove from the heat and leave on one side until the *hanakatsuo* flakes have settled. Strain through a clean cloth and use as required.

It is hard to measure *hanakatsuo* exactly, since it is very light and rather bulky. A handful is about the right quantity for 1 litre ($1\frac{3}{4}$ pints) water and is easier to judge than attempting to measure the flakes on scales or with a spoon.

Dashi with konbu

10 cm (4 inches) *konbu*

Make as directed above, but after removing the *konbu* bring to the boil and lift from the heat without adding the *hanakatsuo*. Use as required without straining.

Soups for all seasons

Soups, like other dishes in Japan, are supposed to reflect the seasons, and the ingredients are always chosen from those which are in season.

Clear soups for spring

Clear soup with somen and quails' eggs

Serves 4

40 g (1½ oz) *somen* (see page 154)
4 quails' eggs or 2 size 6 hens' eggs
800 ml (1⅓ pints) *dashi*
5 ml (1 teaspoon) salt
30 ml (2 tablespoons) *sake*
10 ml (2 teaspoons) soy sauce
12 slices of cucumber, cut 2 mm (1/12 inch) thick

Put the *somen* into a pan of boiling water and boil until just soft (about 5 minutes). Then cool quickly in a strainer under the cold tap and leave to drain. Hard-boil the eggs and shell (if using hens' eggs cut each in half). Mix the *dashi* with the salt and *sake* and bring to the boil. Add the soy sauce and adjust the seasoning to taste. Arrange a portion of *somen* in each soup bowl together with 3 slices of cucumber and an egg. Ladle over the boiling *dashi* and serve at once.

Clear soup with kamaboko and french beans

Serves 4

The original Japanese recipe for this soup suggests using chrysanthemum leaves with the fish paste, but since these are virtually unobtainable in the UK during spring a good substitute would be french beans (from Kenya), which can be bought fresh at this time.

1 packet of *kamaboko*
25 g (1 oz) french beans
800 ml (1⅓ pints) *dashi*
2.5 ml (½ teaspoon) salt
15 ml (1 tablespoon) soy sauce

Slice the *kamaboko* into 12 slices ½ cm (¼ inch) thick. Top and tail the beans and cut into 5-cm (2-inch) lengths. Boil in lightly salted water for 7 minutes, then cool quickly under the cold tap. Drain well. Arrange the *kamaboko* and beans in four soup bowls. Bring the *dashi* to the boil and adjust the seasoning with salt and soy sauce. Pour into the soup bowls and serve at once.

Wuntun and cucumber soup

Serves 4

This soup is Chinese in origin.

Filling for wuntun:
75 g (3 oz) chicken meat, without bones
1 spring onion
1.5 ml (¼ teaspoon) ginger juice
2.5 ml (½ teaspoon) salt

———
12 bought *wuntun* skins
20 g (¾ oz) salted *wakame* or 1 length dried *wakame*
50 g (2 oz) cucumber
600 ml (1 pint) *dashi*
2.5 ml (½ teaspoon) salt
15 ml (1 tablespoon) *sake*
5 ml (1 teaspoon) soy sauce

Mince the chicken and spring onion together very finely, or use a food-processor, then beat the ginger juice and salt into the paste. Divide into twelve and put one portion on the centre of each *wuntun* skin. Gather up the four corners of the skin, then pinch just above the chicken paste to ensure that the top is tightly closed. Drop the *wuntun* into a pan of boiling water and boil for 5 minutes, or until they rise to the top. Then lift out with a slotted spoon and set aside to drain. Soak the *wakame* in cold water for 5 minutes, then discard the hard edgeand cut into 2-cm (¾-inch) lengths. Wash the cucumber and with a small spoon hollow out the seeds, leaving the cucumber flesh as a ring, then cut into 2 mm ($\frac{1}{10}$ inch)-thick slices. Bring the *dashi* to the boil and season to taste with salt, *sake*• and soy sauce. Add the *wuntun*, cucumber rings and *wakame*. Bring back to the boil and serve immediately.

Clear soups for summer

Clear soup with aubergines and spring onions

Serves 4

100 g (4 oz) aubergine
4 spring onions (white only)
800 ml (1⅓ pints) *dashi*
sugar, salt and soy sauce to taste

Cut the aubergine into 12 slices and soak for 20 minutes in cold water to remove any bitterness. Cut the onion white into long, hair-like shreds. Drain the aubergine and put it into a bowl with the *dashi*. Stand the bowl in a steamer and steam over a high heat for 35 minutes. Lift out the aubergine slices, reserving the *dashi*, and arrange in four heated soup bowls with the shredded onion. Keep warm. Put the reserved *dashi* into a saucepan and bring to the boil. Season to taste with sugar, salt and soy sauce, then pour over the aubergine and onion and serve immediately.

Clear soup with okra

Serves 4

50 g (2 oz) okra
800 ml (1⅓ pints) *dashi*
4 slices of ginger
soy sauce and salt to taste

Run a knife up and down the skin of the okra pods to remove some of their down, taking care not to cut the skin. Rinse well and put into boiling salted water for 5 minutes. Refresh in cold water, then cut into 2-cm (¾-inch) lengths, discarding the stalks. Bring the *dashi* to the boil and add the ginger and okra. Continue boiling for a few seconds and season to taste with soy sauce and salt. Serve in four heated soup bowls.

Another version of this soup can be made with 150 g (5 oz) silk beancurd. Cut the beancurd into 1½-cm (½-inch) cubes and carefully slide about three into each heated soup bowl. Immediately ladle over the boiling soup with the okra and ginger and serve.

Clear soup with cucumber

Serves 4

50 g (2 oz) cucumber
800 ml (1⅓ pints) *dashi*
5 ml (1 teaspoon) sugar
15 ml (1 tablespoon) *sake*
2.5 ml (½ teaspoon) salt
10 ml (2 teaspoons) soy sauce

Cut the cucumber into thin slices and arrange a few in each pre-heated soup bowl. Bring the *dashi* to the boil and season carefully, tasting between each addition. Then pour the *dashi* over the cucumber slices and serve at once.

Clear soups for autumn

Chrysanthemum flower clear soup

Serves 4

4 small yellow edible chrysanthemum flowers*
4 dried mushrooms
1 small celery heart
800 ml (1⅓ pints) *dashi*
2.5 ml (½ teaspoon) salt
30 ml (2 tablespoons) *sake*
10 ml (2 teaspoons) soy sauce

Tear the petals from the chrysanthemum flowers and rinse gently in cold water. Blanch in boiling water for 30 seconds, then refresh under the cold tap. Leave to drain. Wash and soak the dried mushrooms in

---

* The edible chrysanthemum plant (see page 172) flowers very freely in the late summer and autumn. Pick the flower heads when they first open.

150 ml (¼ pint) warm water for 30 minutes; then, reserving the soaking water, discard the hard stem and cut the caps into thin slices. Simmer gently in the reserved soaking water for 5 minutes, then drain well. Cut the celery heart with the leaves into narrow lengths. Bring the *dashi* to the boil and season with salt, *sake* and soy sauce, tasting between each addition. Arrange the chrysanthemum petals, mushroom slices and celery strips in four pre-heated soup bowls. Pour the *dashi* into the bowls and serve at once.

Mushroom and egg soup

Serves 4

75 g (3 oz) young leeks
2 dried mushrooms
800 ml (1⅓ pints) *dashi*
4 ml (¾ teaspoon) salt
5 ml (1 teaspoon) soy sauce

Thickening paste:
5 ml (1 teaspoon) potato flour
15 ml (1 tablespoon) water

---

1 egg, beaten

Cut the leeks into 2-mm ($\frac{1}{10}$-inch) rings and wash very well in a strainer. Soak the dried mushrooms in warm water for 30 minutes, then discard the hard stalks and cut the caps into thin slices. Put the *dashi* and the mushrooms into a pan and bring to the boil. Add the seasonings and dribble in the potato-flour paste, stirring all the time. While the soup is gently boiling add the leek rings and the beaten egg. Mix well and remove from the heat. Serve in individual heated soup bowls.

Clear soup with silk beancurd and spinach

Serves 4

150 g (5 oz) silk beancurd
50 g (2 oz) fresh spinach leaves
800 ml (1⅓ pints) *dashi*
2.5 ml (½ teaspoon) salt
10 ml (2 teaspoons) soy sauce
wasabi mustard

Cut the silk beancurd into four equal squares and carefully slide one into each soup bowl. Wash the spinach leaves and tear away any tough centre veins. Par-boil in lightly salted water for 2 minutes, then immediately refresh under the cold tap. Drain well. Bring the *dashi* to the boil and season with the salt and soy sauce. Arrange a few spinach leaves in each soup bowl with the beancurd and put a dab of *wasabi* mustard on the pieces of beancurd. Pour over the boiling *dashi* and serve immediately.

Clear soups for winter

Chicken and white radish soup

Serves 4

175 g (6 oz) chicken breast
15 ml (1 tablespoon) *sake*
1.5 ml (¼ teaspoon) salt
50 g (2 oz) white radish
sugar, salt and soy sauce to taste
20 ml (4 teaspoons) finely chopped spring onion

Skin the chicken and remove any fat. Cut the breast into triangular-shaped pieces about 2 cm (¾ inch) long. Marinate in the *sake* and salt for 20 minutes. Grate the white radish and squeeze dry in a clean cloth. Put the chicken and the marinade into 900 ml (1½ pints) boiling water, and over a moderate heat skim the surface until the scum has stopped rising to the top. Then turn down the heat and gently simmer the chicken for about 10 minutes. Lift out the chicken pieces and keep warm. Season the stock to taste with sugar, salt and soy sauce. Arrange the chicken pieces in four pre-heated bowls. Add 5 ml (1 teaspoon) white radish pulp to each bowl and sprinkle over with the finely chopped spring onion. Carefully pour the boiling stock into each bowl without disturbing the arrangement of chicken and white radish and serve at once.

Clear soup with sea bass steaks

Serves 4

2 slices of sea bass, each 3 cm (1 inch) thick
800 ml (1⅓ pints) *dashi*
2.5 ml (½ teaspoon) salt
2.5 ml (½ teaspoon) caster sugar
10 ml (2 teaspoons) soy sauce
4 spring onions (green only)
1 small sheet *nori*

Gently poach the sea bass steaks in lightly salted water until cooked. Then drain, divide each in half, discarding the bones, and keep warm. Bring the *dashi* to the boil and season to taste with salt, sugar and soy sauce. Cut the green parts of the spring onion into 4-cm (1½-inch) lengths, and the *nori* into thin shreds. Arrange a portion of sea bass together with some onion and shredded *nori* in each pre-heated soup bowl. Pour over the boiling *dashi* without disturbing the arrangement and serve at once.

Miso soups

Red *Miso* is the standard type of *miso* used in both breakfast and dinner soups, although sometimes, particularly in winter, the darker *hatcho miso* is used. Red *miso* is saltier than white *miso*, which is often rather sweet, while *hatcho miso* has a much stronger, saltier flavour than ordinary red *miso*. Since not all *miso* flavours are to Western taste, and the different brands, quite apart from the different types, vary in their texture and strength of flavour, it is worthwhile experimenting to find the one which most appeals to you. Unless the recipe specifies red or white *miso*, use whichever you prefer. However, whatever kind of *miso* is used it must be very thoroughly blended with a small quantity of *dashi* before it is added to the main body of the soup, otherwise it will become lumpy. If *miso* is boiled its flavour will change, so it should always be added at the last minute, just before serving.

Garnish ingredients that require cooking can be cooked in the *dashi* before the *miso* is added, but soft ingredients such as beancurd, *wakame* and cucumber should be put directly into the soup bowls and the hot soup ladled over them. The choice of ingredients for garnishes is endless, for almost any seasonal vegetable can be used. There are no hard and fast rules and cooks are free to use their own ingenuity to create an infinite variety of *miso* soups.

Miso soups for spring

Miso soup with silk beancurd and wakame

Serves 4

40 g (1½ oz) salted *wakame*, or 2 lengths dried *wakame*
300 g (10 oz) silk beancurd
800 ml (1⅓ pints) *dashi*
60 ml (4 tablespoons) red *miso*

Rinse the *wakame*, then soak in cold water for 5 minutes. Trim off the tough edge and cut the leaves into bite-sized pieces. Scald with boiling water, refresh immediately in cold water, then drain. Cut the beancurd into 16 cubes and carefully place four in each heated soup bowl together with the *wakame*. Bring the *dashi* to the boil, then take out about half a teacupful to mix with the *miso*. Blend very thoroughly together in a small bowl, then pour back into the boiling *dashi*. Lift from the heat at once and ladle over the beancurd and *wakame*. Serve immediately.

Miso soup with shellfish

Serves 4

In Japan this soup is made with a variety of small clams that can be bought live at most fishmongers. In the UK, since it has become increasingly difficult to buy either live cockles or live 'carpet shells' (the French *palourdes*), compromise is usually necessary. Live mussels may be used, but they are at best a poor substitute for the real thing. If using either clams or cockles soak in salted water overnight to allow them to purge themselves. If using mussels, sprinkle with a handful of dry oatmeal and leave overnight in a dark, cool place.

350 g (12 oz) live cockles
60 ml (4 tablespoons) red *miso*

Wash the shellfish very thoroughly after they have been left to clean themselves overnight. Discard any that remain open after washing. Put into 800 ml (1⅓ pints) boiling water and bring back to the boil. *Discard any shellfish that remain closed*. If using mussels, leave overnight sprinkled with oatmeal, wash very thoroughly in several lots of water and tear off their beards. Discard any that remain open during the washing. Put into 800 ml (1⅓ pints) cold water and bring slowly to the boil. Boil for 2 minutes and discard any mussels that remain closed.

Skim the water and remove about half a teacupful to mix with the *miso*. When the *miso* is well blended, pour into the pan and bring just to the boil. Remove from the heat and serve in separate soup bowls.

Miso soup with egg and spring onions

Serves 4

4 spring onions (green only)
4 egg yolks
800 ml (1⅓ pints) *dashi*
60 ml (4 tablespoons) *miso*

Cut the green parts of the spring onions into 4-cm (1½-inch) lengths. Arrange with the egg yolks in four soup bowls, taking care not to break the yolks. Mix 100 ml (3½ fl oz) of the *dashi* with the *miso* into a smooth paste. Bring the rest of the *dashi* to the boil and stir in the *miso*. Lift from the heat and immediately pour over the egg yolks. Serve at once.

Miso soups for summer

Miso soup with beancurd and spinach

Serves 4

150 g (5 oz) cotton beancurd
50 g (2 oz) fresh leaf spinach
800 ml (1⅓ pints) *dashi*
60 ml (4 tablespoons) red *miso*

Cut the beancurd into 1-cm (½-inch) cubes. Wash the spinach and tear out any tough centre veins. Cook in boiling water for 4 minutes, then refresh in cold water before cutting into 4-cm (1½-inch) lengths and draining. Heat the *dashi*, reserving about 100 ml (3½ fl oz) to mix with the *miso*. When the *dashi* is hot, stir in the well-blended *miso* and add the beancurd cubes. Continue to cook over a very low heat for another 3 minutes, without boiling. Add the spinach and serve immediately in separate heated soup bowls.

Beancurd balls with miso soup

Serves 4

150 g (5 oz) cotton beancurd
30 ml (2 tablespoons) potato flour or arrowroot
pinch of salt
8 broad beans, par-boiled and skinned, or 10 ml (2 teaspoons) cooked peas
5 ml (1 teaspoon) black sesame seeds
oil for deep frying
800 ml (1⅓ pints) *dashi* made with *konbu*
60 ml (4 tablespoons) *miso*

Wrap the beancurd tightly in a towel and press under a board for about 2 hours. Then mash with the potato flour and a pinch of salt until smooth, leaving the sides of the bowl clean. Very finely chop the beans or peas into minute pieces and mix with the sesame seeds into the beancurd paste. Heat the oil to about 150°C (300°F). Oil the hands and squeeze the paste between the thumb and forefinger to make small balls the size of marbles, or roll the paste between the hands to shape the balls. Deep-fry for about 5 minutes, then put on one side to drain. Reserve 100 ml (3½ fl oz) of the *dashi* and bring the rest to the boil. Drop in the beancurd balls to re-heat. Blend the *miso* with the reserved *dashi* and stir into the soup. Remove from the heat and serve.

Miso soups for autumn

Miso soup with white radish and wakame

Serves 4

60 g (2½ oz) white radish
25 g (1 oz) carrot
10 g (½ oz) salted *wakame* or
1 length dried *wakame*
800 ml (1⅓ pints) *dashi*
60 ml (4 tablespoons) *miso*

Peel the white radish and cut into matchsticks about 4 cm (1½ inches) long. Peel the carrot and cut into similar-shaped lengths. Wash the *wakame* and soak in cold water for 5 minutes before removing the hard edge and cutting the leaf into pieces. Bring the *dashi* to the boil, reserving 100 ml (3½ fl oz) to mix with the *miso*, and cook the white radish and carrot sticks in the *dashi* for about 5 minutes. Blend the *miso* with the reserved *dashi* and stir into the soup. Add the *wakame* and serve at once without letting the *miso* boil.

Miso soup with marrow and leek

Serves 4

180 g (6 oz) marrow
1 small leek
800 ml (1⅓ pints) *dashi*
60 ml (4 tablespoons) *miso*

Peel and cut the marrow into slices about 1½ cm (½ inch) thick. Remove the seeds. Wash and trim the leek and cut into rings about ½ cm (¼ inch) thick. Simmer the marrow in the *dashi* for about 5 minutes, then add the leek and continue cooking for another 3 minutes. Take about half a teacupful of the *dashi* from the pan to mix with the *miso*. When the *miso* has been blended into a smooth, thin paste, stir into the soup. Bring the soup just up to boiling point again and serve at once.

Miso soup with yams, spring onions and white radish

Serves 4

180 g (6 oz) small yams
800 ml (1⅓ pints) *dashi*
50 g (2 oz) white radish
4 spring onions (green only)
60 ml (4 tablespoons) *miso*

Peel the yams thickly and rub with a little salt to remove some of their stickiness, then rinse well. Put into cold water and bring to the boil. Boil for 5 minutes, then rinse and change the water. Bring back to the boil and boil for 3 minutes, then drain and rinse again. Now put into the *dashi* and simmer gently for 15 minutes, or until just soft. Meanwhile peel and grate the white radish, then squeeze dry in a clean cloth. Cut the green parts of the spring onions into 4-cm (1½-inch) lengths. When the yams are cooked remove from the *dashi* and cut into ½-cm (¼-inch)-thick slices. Arrange with the spring onions and a mound of grated white radish in warmed soup bowls. Remove half a teacupful of the *dashi* and mix with the *miso* into a smooth paste. Stir this paste into the *dashi*, bring just up to boiling point again and ladle over the vegetables in the soup bowls. Serve immediately.

Miso soups for winter

Miso soup with beancurd and mixed vegetables

Serves 4

150 g (5 oz) cotton beancurd
100 g (4 oz) potatoes
2 dried mushrooms
40 g (1½ oz) salsify or scorzonera
100 g (4 oz) white radish
50 g (2 oz) carrot
30 ml (2 tablespoons) oil
600 ml (1 pint) *dashi*
45 ml (3 tablespoons) red *miso*, or *hatcho miso* for a stronger, saltier taste

Wrap the beancurd tightly in a towel and leave for about an hour to drain. Scrape the potatoes and leave to soak in salty water for 5 minutes. Soak the dried mushrooms in warm water for 30 minutes, then discard the hard stalks and cut the caps into thin slices. Peel and shave the salsify into very thin flakes under water to prevent it discolouring. Slice the white radish, carrot and potato into thin oblongs about 3 × 4 cm (1 × 1½ inches). Cut the beancurd into similar-sized slices. Heat the oil in a saucepan and stir-fry the salsify, mushrooms and carrot over a moderate heat for about 2 minutes. Then add the *dashi*, potato and white radish and simmer for 15 minutes. When all the vegetables are cooked, slide in the beancurd, and take out about 100 ml (3½ fl oz) of the stock to mix with the *miso*. When the *miso* is smooth and well blended, pour into the soup. Bring the soup just up to boiling point and serve.

Miso soup with chicken and Chinese leaves

Serves 4

100 g (4 oz) chicken breast
10 ml (2 teaspoons) *sake*
75 g (3 oz) Chinese leaves
25 g (1 oz) carrot
800 ml (1⅓ pints) *dashi*
60 ml (4 tablespoons) *miso*

Sprinkle the chicken breast with the *sake* and place on a plate in a steamer. Steam for 20 minutes, then allow to cool. Remove the skin and cut the meat into bite-sized pieces. Meanwhile wash the Chinese leaves and dip in boiling water for 2 minutes. Refresh in cold water, drain and cut into 5-cm (2-inch) strips. Peel the carrot and cut into flower-shaped slices about ½ cm (¼ inch) thick. Par-boil in lightly salted water for about 5 minutes, then drain. Bring the *dashi* to the boil, reserving 100 ml (3½ fl oz) to mix with the *miso*. Add the chicken, carrot and Chinese leaves to the soup and allow to heat through while mixing the *miso* and reserved *dashi* to a smooth paste. Stir the blended *miso* into the soup, bring just up to the boil, and lift from the heat. Serve at once.

Sweet potato and wakame soup

Serves 4

This recipe is an alternative version of the well-known recipe for MISO SOUP WITH BEANCURD AND WAKAME (page 136).

180 g (6 oz) sweet potato
40 g (1½ oz) salted *wakame* or 2 lengths dried *wakame*
800 ml (1⅓ pints) *dashi*
60 ml (4 tablespoons) red *miso*

Peel the sweet potato and cut into regular-shaped batons about 5 × 1 cm (2 × ½ inch). Simmer in the *dashi* for about 15 minutes, or until just soft. Rinse the *wakame* and soak in cold water for 5 minutes. Then remove the hard edge and cut the soft leaf into short lengths. When the sweet potato is cooked take out about half a teacupful of the *dashi* and mix with the *miso* into a smooth paste. Stir into the soup, add the *wakame* and bring just to the boil. Remove from the heat and serve immediately.

Rice and noodles

Rice, undeniably Japan's most important food, has been the main staple for many centuries. Today, paddy fields still dominate the agricultural landscape. Rice used to be as much part of religion in Japan as bread and wine is in the Christian world, and it remains a major ingredient in festival foods such as red rice and rice cakes, traditional festival offerings at Buddhist temples and Shinto shrines. *Sake*, the national alcoholic drink, is based on rice, and for many hundreds of years rice was the unit of commercial currency and yardstick by which wealth was judged. The original fortunes behind some of the great commerical and industrial names in Japan today, such as Mitsukoshi, the department store company, were built on rice, and in modern Japan it remains a live political issue: over-production has resulted in vast stores of unsold rice, so the government has had to levy taxes for agricultural subsidies to maintain the farmers' incomes.

Noodles, on the other hand, inspire popular pride, and symbolize long life and enduring relationships. Visitors from abroad are taken to taste the noodles of particular noodle-houses, and in some of these, and certain department stores, chefs may be seen demonstrating their skills in the preparation of noodles (and other foods). Such a display often attracts a crowd of onlookers as the chef deftly cuts the dough without any perceptible pause between the down-strokes of his knife. Noodles are judged for their cut and texture as well as for their flavour: a slight unevenness showing the hand-made element in their cutting is much admired. Yet at the same time noodles are the ultimate quick lunch dish everywhere in Japan, and are never eaten as the staple in a main meal.

Plain boiled rice

The standard allowance of rice in Japan is 130 g (4½ oz) per person. In the West, however, 300 g (10 oz) is usually sufficient for 4 people. It is a matter of personal taste and capacity: the proportions of rice and water remain the same: 5 parts rice to 6 parts water. Most families in Japan use an electric rice-cooker, which will automatically boil, dry and keep the rice warm until required. Rice-cookers can be bought in the UK.

300 g (10 oz) Japanese short-grained rice
440 ml (16 fl oz) cold water

Wash the rice very thoroughly in several lots of clean water, using a wire whisk (or, even better, a wooden one), to beat out any loose starch. When the water runs clean, drain the rice and add to the measured water. Leave to soak for about 30 minutes, then bring quickly to the boil. Cover with a lid, reduce the heat and boil for 5 minutes, or until all the water has gone. Then turn down the heat to its very lowest and leave the rice, still covered, to dry for 15 minutes. Finally, turn off the heat and leave the rice for another 10 minutes before serving.

Store left-over cooked rice covered in the refrigerator. To re-heat, add 15 ml (1 tablespoon) water to each 250 g (8 oz) cooked rice and put it, closely covered, in a pre-heated oven (190°C, 375°F, Gas 5) for 20 minutes. Alternatively, re-heat in a steamer.

The starchy water obtained from washing rice can be used for the initial cooking of root vegetables such as white radish or turnips. Wash the rice in one lot of water and discard, then cover again with clean water. Beat the rice well to free the starch, then drain off the water and reserve for cooking vegetables.

Japanese rice balls

Rice rolled into different shapes and flavoured with sour plums (*umeboshi*, see page 167), seaweed or *hanakatsuo* (see page 165) makes a popular cold luncheon or picnic dish in Japan.

Take hot, freshly cooked Japanese short-grained rice and measure about 45 ml (3 tablespoons) into a bowl. Put an *umeboshi* in the middle and cover with another 30 ml (2 tablespoons) rice. Dampen the hands and put a pinch of salt on the palm of the left hand. Roll the rice between the hands, pressing firmly to make a solid ball, but without squashing the grains of rice. Keep on rolling and squeezing until a firm mass results. Then using the flattened palm of the left hand, and with the fingers and palm of the right hand held at a right angle, squeeze the rice ball into a triangle. Shift it round and squeeze again until a neat three-sided shape is obtained with a flat top and bottom. Cut two squares of *nori* and decorate the top and bottom of the rice triangle with these.

Alternatively, roll the rice with the *umeboshi* into a fat sausage, about 7 cm (3 inches) long, and wind a strip of *nori* round its middle.

Make a different rice ball, without the *umeboshi*, by adding 5 ml (1 teaspoon) *hanakatsuo* to the rice and then rolling it into a triangle. Decorate with a square of *nori* top and bottom.

Yet another rice ball can be made from plain rice shaped into a flattened round, rather like a rissole, and cooked in an ungreased frying-pan over a low heat until golden brown on both sides. One side is then painted with a mixture of equal parts of white *miso* and caster sugar and put under the grill for a few moments. These rice balls may be served either hot or cold.

A selection of these different types of rice ball can be served as a cold luncheon dish or taken on a picnic. The Japanese usually arrange these in lunch boxes, often made of highly coloured lacquer.

Chicken with rice and mixed vegetables

Serves 4

This and the following recipe are different versions of rice cooked with chicken and vegetables that can be served in place of plain boiled rice at a main meal, usually for guests or on a special occasion. Salsify and scorzonera are suggested as substitutes for Japanese burdock.

225 g (7½ oz) Japanese short-grained rice
50 g (2 oz) salsify or scorzonera
75 g (3 oz) carrot
3 dried mushrooms
150 g (5 oz) chicken meat, without bones
1 cake of *aburage* (see page 106)
15 ml (1 tablespoon) soy sauce
15 ml (1 tablespoon) *sake*
15 ml (1 tablespoon) caster sugar
2.5 ml (½ teaspoon) salt

Wash the rice very thoroughly in several lots of clean water, beating with a wire whisk to shake free any loose starch. Drain and put aside. Peel or scrape the salsify or scorzonera clean and cut into shavings, turning the vegetable between each cut. Keep in water until required.

Peel the carrot and cut into matchsticks about 3 cm (1 inch) long. Soak the dried mushrooms in hot water for 30 minutes, then discard the hard stalks and cut the caps into thin slices. Cut the chicken into 1-cm (½-inch) cubes. Pour boiling water over the *aburage* to remove any oiliness and cut into thin slices about 3 cm (1 inch) long. Mix the chicken with the soy sauce. Cook over a low heat for 3 minutes, stirring all the time. Then add the *sake* and sugar and remove from the heat. Mix in the vegetables and *aburage*. Put the rice in a big pan, together with 340 ml (12 fl oz) cold water. Put the chicken and mixed vegetables on top and cover with a tight-fitting lid. Cook over a high heat until the water boils, then turn down the heat and cook for another 10 minutes until all the water has gone. Turn off the heat and leave the pan, still tightly covered, for another 10 minutes before serving. Mix the chicken and vegetables into the rice before serving in separate rice bowls.

Chicken with rice

Serves 4

2 dried mushrooms
100 g (4 oz) chicken, without bones
25 ml (5 teaspoons) soy sauce
40 g (1½ oz) carrot
300 g (10 oz) Japanese short-grained rice
10 ml (2 teaspoons) *sake*
5 ml (1 teaspoon) salt
25 g (1 oz) peas (frozen)
2 small eggs
pinch of salt
2.5 ml (½ teaspoon) oil

Soak the dried mushrooms in hot water for 30 minutes, then discard the hard stems and cut the caps into thin slices. Cut the chicken into 2-cm (¾-inch) cubes, sprinkle with 5 ml (1 teaspoon) soy sauce and leave to marinate for 20 minutes. Peel the carrot and cut into matchsticks. Wash the rice very thoroughly in several lots of clean water, beating with a wire whisk to shake free any loose starch. Put into a heavy pan with 450 ml (16 fl oz) cold water. Add the *sake*, 20 ml (4 teaspoons) soy sauce and the salt. Put the chicken, mushrooms and carrot on top of the rice, cover with a close-fitting lid and bring to the boil over a high heat. Immediately it boils, turn down the heat and simmer for about 10 minutes, until all the liquid has gone. Then turn off the heat and leave the rice to dry for another 10 minutes, without lifting the lid. Meanwhile put the peas into boiling water for 3 minutes, then drain well. Beat the eggs with a pinch of salt. Heat a pan with the oil and scramble the eggs over a high heat until dry and crumbly. Just before serving, add the peas to the rice pan and mix the chicken and vegetables into the rice. Divide the rice between four bowls and garnish with the scrambled eggs.

Red rice

Serves 4

This is a traditional Japanese dish, probably dating from the eighth century (it is mentioned in a Chinese poem of that date). Red is a festival colour and red rice is still made for special festivals, marriages and birthdays; at these times it may be presented at the household shrine, as well as being part of a meal. In Japan red rice can be bought freshly made in some supermarkets. Traditionally it is cooked by steaming the rice and beans together, but in this simpler version they are boiled. No plain rice would be served in a meal that includes red rice.

180 g (6 oz) glutinous rice
40 ml (2½ tablespoons) red *adzuki* beans (see page 168)
5 ml (1 teaspoon) black sesame seeds
2.5 ml (½ teaspoon) salt

Wash the rice very thoroughly, drain and leave for an hour. Meanwhile put the beans on to boil in plain water. Boil for 3 minutes, drain, then put into 1 litre (1⅔ pints) fresh cold water. Bring to the boil again and boil until three-quarters cooked – soft but still granular in texture (about 45 minutes). Strain the beans, reserving the water, and keep covered in a bowl to prevent drying out. Make up the bean water to 200 ml (⅓ pint) with fresh water if necessary, and add to the rice. Leave the rice to soak for another 30 minutes, then mix in the beans and bring quickly to the boil. Cover and boil gently for about 7–10 minutes, until all the water has gone, then turn off the heat and leave the rice and beans to dry for 10 minutes, with the lid on. Serve.

Oyako donburi

Serves 4

This is a family luncheon dish that would never be served when entertaining guests. It is sold in almost all the noodle-houses and lunchtime restaurants in urban Japan. The name *oyako* translates as 'parent and child', a reference to the egg and chicken in the dish.

100 g (4 oz) chicken breast

Marinade:
2.5 ml (½ teaspoon) *sake*
2.5 ml (½ teaspoon) soy sauce

---

50 g (2 oz) white of leek
2 dried mushrooms
300 g (10 oz) Japanese short-grained rice

Simmering stock:
150 ml (¼ pint) *dashi* or chicken stock
7.5 ml (1½ teaspoons) soy sauce
15 ml (1 tablespoon) *mirin*
7.5 ml (1½ teaspoons) caster sugar
15 ml (1 tablespoon) *sake*

---

2 size 1 eggs, beaten

Cut the chicken into 2-cm (¾-inch) cubes and marinate for 15 minutes. Wash and trim the leek and cut into long, thin slices, holding the knife at an oblique angle to the leek. Soak the mushrooms in hot water for 30 minutes, then discard the hard stalk and cut the caps into thin slices. Wash the rice very thoroughly, then beat with a wire whisk to shake free any loose starch. Drain well and put into 450 ml (16 oz) cold water and bring quickly to the boil. Cover, and turn down the heat and boil for 10 minutes until all the water has gone. Then, still covered, turn off the heat and leave to dry for another 10 minutes. Meanwhile put the mushrooms, leeks and chicken into the simmering stock and bring to the boil. Simmer for 4–5 minutes, then pour the beaten eggs on top. Cover the pan and simmer until the eggs are half-cooked (about 3 minutes). Then turn off the heat and leave the pan covered while the eggs finish cooking in the heat of the liquid. When the rice is ready, divide between four deep bowls and cover each with a quarter of the egg-and-chicken mixture. Offer seven-spice pepper as an optional extra seasoning.

Sushi

Serves 4

Most people who have visited Japan associate *sushi* with *sashimi* (raw fish), for which it is difficult to buy really fresh ingredients in the UK. Even in Japan housewives do not try to reproduce the kinds of raw fish with *sushi* dishes made by professional *sushi* chefs. *Sushi* itself is vinegared rice, made by mixing a vinegar dressing into hot rice which is cooled by fanning during the mixing. *Sushi* rice made at home is garnished with vegetables. These simple *sushi* are served either in a main meal, in which case no plain rice is served, or on their own for a luncheon.

2 large dried mushrooms

Stock for mushrooms:
15 ml (1 tablespoon) soy sauce
15 ml (1 tablespoon) *mirin*
25 ml (1½ tablespoons) caster sugar
pinch of salt

---

5 g (¼ oz) dried winter melon strips
1.5 ml (¼ teaspoon) salt

Stock for winter melon strips:
200 ml (⅓ pint) *dashi* or water
15 ml (1 tablespoon) caster sugar
15 ml (1 tablespoon) soy sauce
15 ml (1 tablespoon) *mirin*

---

1 egg
125 g (4 oz) cucumber
3 slices of pickled ginger (see page 158) (optional)
300 g (10 oz) Japanese short-grained rice
400 ml (14 fl oz) water

Dressing for rice:
40 ml (2½ tablespoons) rice vinegar
30 ml (2 tablespoons) caster sugar
3.5 ml (¾ teaspoon) salt

---

4 large sheets of *nori*

Wash and soak the mushrooms in 200 ml ($\frac{1}{3}$ pint) warm water for 30 minutes, then discard the hard stalks and put the caps with the soaking water into a pan. Bring to the boil and add the soy sauce, *mirin*, caster sugar and salt. Simmer until almost dry, then leave to cool before cutting into slices $\frac{1}{2}$ cm ($\frac{1}{5}$ inch) wide.

Wash and rub the winter melon strips with a little salt and rinse well. Put to soak in cold water for 5 minutes, then, in fresh water, boil for 15 minutes. Drain and put the melon strips into a clean pan with 200 ml ($\frac{1}{3}$ pint) *dashi* or water and 15 ml (1 tablespoon) caster sugar. Simmer until the melon is soft, then add the soy sauce and *mirin*. Continue boiling until the melon is very soft, adding more water if necessary. When the melon is cooked, lay the strips flat and cut into lengths 18 cm (7 inches) long. Cut the lengths into strips about $\frac{1}{2}$ cm ($\frac{1}{5}$ inch) wide.

Beat the egg and make into an unseasoned omelette in a lightly greased pan. When the egg is just set on top, roll up the omelette and put on a plate to cool. Cut into $\frac{1}{2}$-cm ($\frac{1}{5}$-inch) strips lengthways.

Wash and cut the cucumber lengthways into quarters. Remove the seeds and cut the flesh into batons about $\frac{1}{2}$ cm ($\frac{1}{5}$ inch) square and 15 cm (6 inches) long.

Cut the pickled ginger into very fine shreds.

(All this preparation can be done well in advance of the meal.)

Wash the rice very thoroughly in several lots of cold water, beating with a whisk to shake free any loose starch. When the washing water runs clean, drain well and leave to soak for 30 minutes with 400 ml (14 fl oz) cold water. Then quickly bring to the boil, cover and boil over a reduced heat for 5 minutes, or until all the water has gone. Turn the heat down to its very lowest and leave the rice, still covered, to dry for 15 minutes. Meanwhile mix the vinegar dressing. When the rice has finished cooking, turn out into a large bowl and sprinkle the dressing over it. Work this into the rice with a spatula in a figure-of-eight movement, and at the same time fan it vigorously, or use a hand-held hair-dryer set at cold. The rice will become shiny as it cools.

Lay a sheet of *nori* on a rolling mat and cover with a layer of rice, leaving a bare 3 cm (1 inch) at the top and bottom free of rice. Lay a line of egg strips, cucumber batons, mushroom slices, winter melon strips and shreds of ginger across the centre of the rice. Then using the rolling mat lift the *nori* and rice and roll into a cylinder around the vegetables. It should be about 5 cm (2 inches) in diameter. Repeat twice more to make two more rolls.

Cut the last sheet of *nori* in half and make two thinner rolls with only winter melon strips down the centre of the rice. Finally, just before serving, cut the big rolls into slices about 1 cm ($\frac{1}{2}$ inch) thick and the smaller rolls into 4-cm ($1\frac{1}{2}$-inch) lengths. Arrange on individual plates and serve with little dishes of soy sauce as a dipping sauce.

Crab sushi

Serves 4

Crab *sushi* is usually served instead of plain rice with other dishes in a main meal. It can be made well in advance, then kept covered in the refrigerator until required. It is more common as a summer dish.

4 dried mushrooms
15 ml (1 tablespoon) black fungus
20 ml (4 teaspoons) caster sugar
20 ml (4 teaspoons) soy sauce
7.5 ml (1½ teaspoons) *mirin*
300 ml (10 oz) Japanese short-grained rice
10 ml (2 teaspoons) oil
2 eggs, beaten with a pinch of salt
100 g (4 oz) white crab meat (fresh or frozen)
20 snow peas or french beans

Seasoning sauce for rice:
15 ml (1 tablespoon) caster sugar
5 ml (1 teaspoon) salt
50 ml (3¼ tablespoons) rice vinegar

---

20 ml (4 teaspoons) pickled ginger (see page 158)

Wash the mushrooms and soak in 200 ml (⅓ pint) warm water for 30 minutes. Soak the black fungus in warm water for 15 minutes, then rinse well and cut into thin strips. When the dried mushrooms are soft, discard their hard stalks and boil the caps in the soaking water for 5 minutes. Add the caster sugar and continue boiling for another 3 minutes. Finally, add the soy sauce and *mirin* and cook over a reduced heat until all but 30 ml (2 tablespoons) of the liquid has gone. Reserve this liquor and cut the caps into thin slices. Put the black fungus strips into the reserved mushroom cooking liquor and simmer gently for 3 minutes. Then drain.

Wash the rice very thoroughly in several lots of cold water, beating with a wire whisk to shake free any loose starch. When the washing water runs clear, drain well and leave for 30 minutes. Then add 400 ml (14 fl oz) cold water and bring quickly to the boil. Cover and boil over a reduced heat for about 10 minutes until all the water has gone. Then turn off the heat and leave the rice, covered, to dry for 10 minutes. Meanwhile prepare the rest of the ingredients. Heat a medium-sized frying-pan with the oil. Pour in half the beaten egg and cook as a very thin omelette. When the egg has almost set on top, fold in half and continue cooking for another 20 seconds. Turn out of the pan and leave to cool. Make a second omelette with the remaining egg. When both omelettes are cold, cut into very thin strips. Tear the crab meat into shreds. (If using fresh crab, see instructions on page 125. Dip the fresh meat into salted boiling water for 30 seconds, then drain well.) Top and tail the snow peas and boil in lightly salted water for 5 minutes. Drain and cut diagonally into very thin slices. Mix the seasoning sauce for the rice.

When the rice is ready, stand a big bowl on a damp cloth to hold it steady, and turn the rice out into it. Using a wooden spatula, mix in the seasoning sauce with a figure-of-eight movement, and at the same time fan the rice briskly to cool it as quickly as possible. (A hand-held hair-dryer set at cold may be used instead of a fan.) Add the peas, crab, mushrooms and black fungus, reserving a little of the mushrooms and black fungus for the final garnish. Mix quickly and continue fanning. As the rice cools it will become shiny. Serve cold in individual bowls garnished with the egg, mushrooms, black fungus and pickled ginger.

Stuffed aburage pockets

Serves 4

Though the *sushi* rice and prepared vegetables described in the previous recipe may be used to stuff *aburage* pockets, the recipe below includes an alternative stuffing. These stuffed beancurd bags are served cold, either in a main meal, in which it is unlikely that any plain rice would be served, or as a lunch dish, or taken on a picnic.

6 cakes of *aburage*

Stock for aburage:
300 ml (½ pint) *dashi*
30 ml (2 tablespoons) *sake*
45 ml (3 tablespoons) *mirin*
45 ml (3 tablespoons) caster sugar
60 ml (4 tablespoons) soy sauce

---

5 g (¼ oz) dried winter melon strips
1.5 ml (¼ teaspoon) salt

Stock for winter melon:
200 ml (⅓ pint) *dashi*
15 ml (1 tablespoon) caster sugar
15 ml (1 tablespoon) *mirin*
15 ml (1 tablespoon) soy sauce

---

50 g (2 oz) walnuts
200 g (7½ oz) Japanese short-grained rice

Vinegar dressing for rice:
30 ml (2 tablespoons) rice vinegar
20 ml (4 teaspoons) caster sugar
2.5 ml (½ teaspoon) salt

Cut the *aburage* cakes into halves across, and open each square pouch. Remove any extra soft beancurd from the inside of each pouch and pour boiling water over to remove any excess oiliness. Put the pouches into a pan with the stock for *aburage* and simmer gently until there is no stock left. Use a drop lid to cover while simmering. Then leave to cool. When cool enough to handle very gently turn six of the pockets inside out. Meanwhile prepare the winter melon by washing and rubbing the strips with a little salt, then rinsing well. Put to soak for 5 minutes in cold water, then boil in fresh water for 15 minutes. Drain and put the melon strips into a clean pan with the *dashi* and 15 ml (1 tablespoon) sugar. Bring to the boil and add the *mirin* and soy sauce.

Continue simmering until the melon strips are very soft, adding more water if necessary. When the melon is cooked cut into minute pieces. Chop the walnuts very finely.

Wash the rice very thoroughly in several lots of cold water, beating with a wire whisk to shake free any loose starch. When the washing water runs clear, drain well and leave for 30 minutes. Then put into a pan with 320 ml (11 fl oz) cold water and bring quickly to the boil. Cover and boil over a reduced heat for about 10 minutes until all the water has gone, then turn off the heat and leave, still covered, to dry for 10 minutes. Meanwhile prepare the vinegar dressing. When the rice is cooked turn out into a big bowl standing on a damp cloth and sprinkle the dressing over. Work into the rice using a wooden spatula with a figure-of-eight movement, while fanning vigorously to cool quickly (or use a hand-held hair-dryer). It will become shiny as it cools. Mix in the winter melon and the chopped walnuts. Roll a small portion of this mixture into a ball between the hands and slide into one of the *aburage* pockets. Fasten the pocket by turning in the sides at the top opening and folding over the top flap like an envelope. Take care not to tear the *aburage* skin. Repeat for all 12 pockets, then arrange on four separate plates before serving.

Noodles

There are two kinds of Japanese noodles: those made with buckwheat flour, which are called *soba*, have a slightly peppery taste and a greyish colour; and those made with wheat flour, which are white and called *udon*. The quantities per person will vary according to appetite. In Japan the average helping of dried noodles is about 100 g (3½ oz), but in the UK 75 g (3 oz) dried *soba* noodles and 50–75 g (2–3 oz) dried *udon* would probably be more appropriate.

Fresh soba noodles

Although an extremely simple food, *soba* (buckwheat noodles) are one of the most highly regarded of Japanese traditional foods. Since buckwheat flour contains very little gluten, it is usually mixed with strong white flour. The proportions can be as high as 75 per cent buckwheat, but the resulting dough is very tricky to handle and apt to break. For this reason a mixture of half buckwheat flour, half strong flour is recommended: this is easy to handle and gives a good result. Of course, dried *soba* noodles may be bought ready-made from many healthfood shops as well as from Chinese and Japanese stores. The buckwheat flour sold in healthfood shops in the UK is coarser than that used normally for *soba* in Japan.

180 g (6 oz) buckwheat flour
180 g (6 oz) strong white flour
180 ml (6 fl oz) hot water

Mix the two flours in a bowl and make a well in the middle. Pour in the water and mix to a dough. It should be damp enough to be soft and not crumble, but should not stick to the hands. If necessary add another 5 ml (1 teaspoon) water. Knead very vigorously until the dough is smooth and will bend without cracking or crumbling. Leave in a warm place for 1 hour for the gluten to develop. Divide into two equal portions and on a well-floured board roll out one portion into an oblong shape about 2 mm ($\frac{1}{10}$ inch) thick. Flour the dough evenly and fold in each side edge to meet in the centre. Then fold the dough in half, so that there are four thicknesses in an oblong one-quarter its original width. Cut the dough across the folds into thin strips about 3 mm ($\frac{1}{8}$ inch) wide. Shake very gently to unwind the noodles without breaking them. Leave spread out while making the rest of the noodles. (This dough should not be frozen but will keep for about 48 hours uncooked in the refrigerator.) Cook as directed below.

A pasta-maker can be used to cut well-floured flat sheets of this dough into noodles, but the initial rolling must be done on a floured board with a rolling-pin.

Cooking soba (fresh or dried) Bring a large pan of water to the boil, then lift from the heat so that it is no longer quite boiling and slide in the *soba* noodles. Return to a high heat and, when the water boils and foams, slow down the cooking by pouring in one-third of a cup of cold water. Repeat the boiling and adding cold water 2–3 times. Cook the noodles for 6–7 minutes in all. They should be firm but not hard in the centre: take care not to overcook. When ready, drain in a sieve, then quickly wash under the cold tap. Drain well.

Cold soba

Serves 4

This is usually a summer dish, though some people eat it all the year round.

Sauce:
400 ml ($\frac{2}{3}$ pint) *dashi*
100 ml ($3\frac{1}{2}$ fl oz) soy sauce
100 ml ($3\frac{1}{2}$ fl oz) *mirin*

---

360 g (12 oz) *soba*, cooked
50 g (2 oz) spring onion, finely chopped

Boil the ingredients of the sauce together and allow to cool. Serve the *soba* drained and cold on plates (preferably wicker), together with a soup cup or bowl of the sauce and a small dish of chopped spring onions for each person. To eat the *soba*, mix some of the spring onion into the sauce, then drop a portion of the *soba* into it. Hold the cup in one hand and by a combination of sucking and lifting the noodles with chopsticks eat them from the cup. Continue replenishing the cup with noodles until both the *soba* and the sauce are finished. (It is good manners to eat *soba* with a loud sucking noise.)

Tempura soba

Serves 4

Serve cold *soba* with a small portion of hot fresh *tempura* (see page 56), brought to the table in a separate basket. Dip the *tempura* as well as the noodles in the sauce before eating.

Soba in hot soup

Serves 4

This is usually a winter dish, although there is no hard and fast rule. The two versions of the soup belong to two different traditions: eastern *samurai* cooking and western court cooking.

(1) *Kanto (eastern) soup*:
1600 ml (2⅔ pints) *dashi*
180 ml (6½ fl oz or 12 tablespoons) soy sauce
40 ml (8 teaspoons) *mirin*
20 ml (4 teaspoons) salt
20 ml (4 teaspoons) caster sugar
10 ml (2 teaspoons) *sake*

———

(2) *Kensai (western) soup*:
1600 ml (2⅔ pints) *dashi*
60 ml (4 tablespoons) soy sauce

———

360 g (12 oz) *soba*, cooked
50 g (2 oz) spring onions, finely chopped

Bring the ingredients of the soup (version 1 or 2) to the boil. Re-heat the *soba* by dipping, in a sieve, into boiling water for about 45 seconds. Then drain and divide between four big heated soup bowls. Pour over the boiling soup and garnish with the finely chopped onions.

Any of the alternative additions listed in the hot *udon* soup recipe (page 154) can be eaten with hot *soba* soup.

Fresh udon noodles

Serves 4

Udon are white noodles made from wheat flour. The name '*udon*' denotes the standard wheat noodles; *hiyamugi* is a thinner variety, and *somen* are even thinner. Each is eaten in a different soup. All can be bought dried in Chinese and Japanese shops in the UK, but *udon* are not difficult to make at home and taste much better when fresh. Whatever quantities are used, the proportion of water to flour is, by weight, half to one.

250 g (8 oz) strong white flour
125 ml (4 fl oz) warm water or
 25 ml (1½ tablespoons) beaten egg
 and 100 ml (3½ fl oz) warm water
2.5 ml (½ teaspoon) salt

Put the flour (and egg if used) in a bowl and pour the salted water into a well in the middle. Mix into a dough, then knead very thoroughly until smooth and elastic. Put into a polythene bag and leave in a warm room for 2–3 hours. Then divide the dough in half and, on a well-floured board, roll out one-half into a thin oblong sheet (25 × 30 cm/10 × 12 inches) and about 2 mm ($\frac{1}{10}$ inch) thick. Make sure the dough is well floured, then fold in the two side edges so that they meet in the centre. Then fold in half again so there are four thicknesses of dough in an oblong about one-quarter its original width. Cut across the folds into strips about ½ cm ($\frac{1}{6}$ inch) wide. Shake the noodles out gently and toss into a bowl of flour to keep until required.

A pasta-maker can be used to roll out and cut this dough, but the dough must be well floured between each operation. The dough should not be frozen, but will keep for about 48 hours uncooked in the refrigerator. Cook as directed below.

Cooking udon (fresh or dried) Heat a large pan of water to just below boiling point and add the noodles. Bring quickly to the boil and boil for 5–6 minutes. Do not let these noodles overcook, since they quickly become mushy. Drain well and rinse in cold water to rid of any loose starch. Leave to drain.

Hot udon soup

Serves 4

This is usually a winter dish.

Kanto or Kensai soup (see page 153)
300–360 g (10–12 oz) *udon*, cooked
finely chopped spring onions to garnish
seven-spice pepper

Bring the soup ingredients to the boil. Re-heat the cooked noodles by dipping in boiling water before dividing between four big heated soup bowls. Pour over the boiling soup and garnish with finely chopped spring onions and seven-spice pepper.

Alternative additions for udon *or* soba *noodles*:

Kitsune noodles is a folk dish. Pour boiling water over 2 cakes of *aburage* to remove any oiliness. Cut into thin strips and cook for about 10 minutes in a stock of 100 ml (3½ fl oz) *dashi*, 15 ml (1 tablespoon) caster sugar and 15 ml (1 tablespoon) soy sauce. Put the cooked *aburage* slices on the noodles before pouring over the boiling soup.

Moon noodles is another very simple dish. Break a raw egg over the top of each helping of hot noodles, then quickly pour over the boiling soup. The egg should cook in the heat of the dish.

Tempura noodles includes *tempura* (fried and battered foods), and therefore cannot be considered a simple quick lunch in the way that beancurd or egg noodles are. Allow a small helping of *tempura* for each person (see page 56). Immediately after frying put the pieces of *tempura* on to the hot noodles before pouring over the boiling soup. Serve at once with seven-spice pepper.

'Clever dog' noodles consists of noodles served with the fried batter scraps skimmed from *tempura* oil.

Cold somen soup

Serves 4

This is a summer dish.

Cold sauce:
400 ml (⅔ pint) *dashi*
150 ml (¼ pint) soy sauce
150 ml (¼ pint) *mirin*

---

250 g (8 oz) *somen* or *hiyamugi*
ice cubes

Garnishes:
sliced cucumber, sliced tomatoes, shreds of cooked ham, canned mandarin orange segments, canned cherries

Boil the sauce ingredients together and allow to become quite cold before serving. Cook the *somen* noodles as directed for *udon* and after rinsing divide between four bowls of iced water containing several ice cubes. Garnish each bowl with the cucumber, tomatoes, ham, mandarin oranges and cherries and serve with the cold sauce in soup cups or bowls. Dip the noodles in the sauce before eating.

Pickles and sweets

Among the delights of a Japanese meal are the pickles that accompany the rice. There are innumerable recipes for salt pickles, vinegar pickles and rice bran (fermented) pickles, each with its own subtle, or not so subtle, aroma and flavour. Each region and district has its own particular style of preserving or pickling certain vegetables; some of the recipes are up to a thousand years old, having been handed down through the generations. Unlike those of Western chutneys and piccalillis, the vegetables in Japanese pickles are usually raw. A wide range of ready-made pickled vegetables can be bought in Japanese, and some Chinese, stores in the UK, but the simple pickles that follow can be made easily at home.

Sweet cakes, on the other hand, are never home-made in Japan. Traditional sweets are still made in small local shops, and recipes for some of these appear at the end of this chapter.

Some of the most traditional cakes in Japan are the various kinds of rice cake, some coated with sweet *miso* and then grilled (almost like toffee apples in the West), others filled with red bean-paste. Other traditional cakes can be seen being made at the stalls outside the great temples. For these, sweet batter is cooked in small moulds over a grill, then sandwiched together with sweet bean-paste and sold while still warm.

Pickles

Salt-pickled Chinese cabbage

Time: 12–24 hours before eating

250 g (8 oz) Chinese leaves
15 ml (1 tablespoon) salt
10 ml (2 teaspoons) soy sauce

Sprinkle the salt on the cabbage leaves and press between two plates. Leave for at least 12 hours (preferably 24) in a cool place. Then rinse, squeeze dry, and cut the leaves into 3-cm (1-inch) lengths. Serve in small individual dishes mixed with a little soy sauce.

Salt-pickled cucumber

Time: 2 hours before eating

15 cm (6 inches) cucumber
15 ml (1 tablespoon) salt
10 ml (2 teaspoons) soy sauce
pinch of sugar

Cut the cucumber into quarters lengthways and rub each with the salt. Place on a flat plate, cover with another and press hard for 2 hours. Then rinse and cut each piece into 3-cm (1-inch) lengths. Serve in small dishes mixed with the soy sauce and sugar.

Broccoli pickled with soy sauce and sesame

Time: 3–12 hours before eating

250 g (8 oz) broccoli
30 ml (2 tablespoons) sesame seeds
15 ml (1 tablespoon) dry English mustard
90 ml (6 tablespoons) soy sauce
30 ml (2 tablespoons) *mirin*

Wash and trim the broccoli into small florets. Cook in boiling water until just tender (about 5 minutes). Then refresh under cold water and drain well. Toast the sesame seeds in a dry pan until golden. Then lightly crush using either a pestle and mortar or a rolling-pin on a board. Mix the dry mustard with the soy sauce and *mirin* and stir in the crushed sesame seeds. Put the broccoli in a bowl and pour this sauce over. Cover and leave to marinate for 3–12 hours before serving in individual small dishes.

Pickled cucumber

Time: up to 24 hours before eating

1 small cucumber
10 ml (2 teaspoons) salt
15 ml (1 tablespoon) English dry mustard
7.5 ml (1½ teaspoons) caster sugar
7.5 ml (1½ teaspoons) moist brown sugar

Put the cucumber on a board and roll in the salt, pressing down firmly. Place with the mustard and sugar in a sealed polythene bag in the refrigerator for 12–24 hours. Then rinse well, slice and serve as an additional small dish at a meal.

Pickled turnip or white radish

Time: 10 days before eating

This recipe makes a crisp pickled turnip. To make it sweeter increase the sugar to 200 g (7 oz) while using the same amount of salt and vinegar. To make a soft sweet pickle use 7.5 ml (1½ teaspoons) salt, 135 ml (4½ fl oz) rice vinegar and 90 g (3 oz) sugar.

500 g (1 lb) turnip or white radish
25 ml (1½ tablespoons) salt
150 ml (5 fl oz) rice vinegar
150 g (5 oz) caster sugar

Wash and trim the turnip or white radish and cut into thin slices about ½ cm (¼ inch) wide. Put in a glass dish and sprinkle with salt. Mix, making sure all the slices are well salted, and leave for 24 hours in a cool place. Then drain well and squeeze dry in a clean cloth, but do not rinse. Put the vinegar and sugar in a saucepan and bring to the boil. Put the white turnip or white radish in a clean screw-topped jar and pour over the vinegar and sugar. Fasten the lid and leave in the refrigerator for at least 10 days before eating. This pickle will keep for about a month in the refrigerator.

Pickled ginger

Time: at least 24 hours before eating

125 g (4 oz) fresh ginger
20 ml (4 teaspoons) salt
100 ml (3½ fl oz) rice vinegar
30 ml (2 tablespoons) caster sugar
a few drops edible red colouring or beetroot juice (optional)

Peel the ginger and cut into thin, vertical slices (with the grain). Blanch in boiling water for 2 minutes, then drain and put into 300 ml (½ pint) cold water with 20 ml (4 teaspoons) salt. Soak for 1 hour. Meanwhile mix the vinegar and sugar in a pan and boil to dissolve the sugar. Allow to cool. Drain the ginger and mix with the vinegar and sugar and colouring (if used). Cover and leave in the refrigerator for at least 24 hours before using. This pickled ginger will keep for months covered in the refrigerator.

Hot cucumber pickle

Time: 1 hour before eating

13 cm (5 inches) cucumber
1 dried chilli
5 ml (1 teaspoon) sesame oil

Seasoning sauce:
5 ml (1 teaspoon) soy sauce
5 ml (1 teaspoon) rice vinegar
5 ml (1 teaspoon) caster sugar
1.5 ml (¼ teaspoon) salt

Cut the cucumber into quarters lengthways and remove the seeds. Then cut each quarter into batons about 1 cm (⅓ inch) wide by 4 cm (1½ inches) long. Cut the chilli into very fine threads. Heat a small frying-pan with the sesame oil over a moderate heat and stir-fry the chilli for 15 seconds. Add the cucumber batons and continue to stir-fry for another 30 seconds. Pour in the seasoning sauce, cook for another 30 seconds, then pour into a clean bowl to cool. Serve divided between four small dishes.

Stuffed cucumber rings

Time: 1 hour before eating

200 g (7 oz) cucumber
7.5 ml (1½ teaspoons) salt
20 g (¾ oz) carrot
40 g (1½ oz) cabbage leaf (any cabbage)
25 g (1 oz) celery
3 × 5 cm (1 × 2 inches) lemon peel

Dressing:
15 ml (1 tablespoon) lemon juice
30 ml (2 tablespoons) rice vinegar
7.5 ml (1½ teaspoons) caster sugar
2.5 ml (½ teaspoon) salt

Roll the cucumber in 5 ml (1 teaspoon) salt on a board, then rinse well. Cut into 8-cm (3-inch) lengths. Scrape out the seeds from the centre of each piece. Peel the carrot and cut into very fine hair-like threads. Remove any tough veins from the cabbage and cut the leaf into fine shreds. Cut the celery and the lemon peel into thin threads. Mix the shredded vegetables together with 2.5 ml (½ teaspoon) salt, then stuff into the hollowed-out cucumber. Lay the lengths of cucumber between two boards and press for 1 hour. Meanwhile mix the dressing. To serve, cut the cucumber into 1-cm (½-inch) lengths and arrange on individual dishes. Pour over the dressing.

Sweets

Japanese sweets hold a middle ground somewhere between cakes and desserts, and are usually eaten with a cup of green tea. There are three basic kinds of 'cakes' in Japan: those made with *agar-agar* and resembling a delicate jelly; those made with glutinous rice, often coating a sweet red-bean paste centre; and those that are made with some form of dough, usually filled with sweet red-bean paste and either steamed or baked.

Sweet red-bean paste

Makes about 350 g (12 oz)

Two types of sweet bean-paste are used in Japanese cake-making: in one the boiled beans are strained as well as mashed, making a very smooth paste, while in the other the boiled beans are only mashed, resulting in a rather coarse-textured paste. The recipe below is for the smooth type of bean-paste. To make a coarse paste, omit the sieving and immediately after mashing squeeze the pulp dry in a cloth bag.

150 g (5 oz) *adzuki* beans
150 g (5 oz) caster sugar
1.5 ml (¼ teaspoon) salt

Wash the beans well and put into a saucepan with 800 ml (1⅓ pints) cold water. Bring to the boil, immediately add 200 ml (⅓ pint) cold water and bring back to the boil over a moderate heat. Drain off the water from the beans, then start again with 1½ litres (2½ pints) tepid water. Bring slowly to the boil over a moderate heat, then, when boiling, cover the pan and reduce the heat. Boil gently until the beans are very soft (about 1½ hours).

When the beans are ready, pour off most of the water and mash. (A potato-masher is useful for this job.) Then pour the mashed beans into a sieve standing in a bowl of clean water. Work the bean pulp through the sieve with a wooden spoon, so that only the hard shells remain in the sieve and the pulp is in suspension in the water. (Or use a *mouli-légumes* with a medium grille.) Discard the hard shells and strain the bean-water through a fine cotton cloth, or better still through a jelly-bag. Squeeze tightly to get rid of as much water as possible. Put one-third of this dried bean pulp into a clean pan with the sugar and over a moderate heat mix with a wooden spoon until the sugar has dissolved. Then add the rest of the bean pulp and continue mixing over the heat until the paste becomes shiny. Add the salt and remove from the heat. Store in a covered container in a cool place until required.

Red-bean jelly

Makes 20 sweets

3.5 g (⅛ oz) *agar-agar* or ½ stick of Japanese *kanten*
350 g (12 oz) sweet red-bean paste
30 ml (2 tablespoons) sugar
1.5 ml (¼ teaspoon) salt

Rinse and soak the *agar-agar* in cold water for 30 minutes. Then squeeze out the soaking water and if necessary tear the *agar-agar* into small pieces. Put into a pan with 300 ml (½ pint) cold water and bring slowly to the boil. Boil gently until the *agar-agar* has dissolved (about 10 minutes) without stirring. Then add the red-bean paste and the sugar and boil for 3 minutes, stirring all the time with a wooden spoon. Add the salt and remove from the heat. Strain immediately into a clean pan, then cool quickly by dipping the pan into cold water for about 1 minute. Have ready a tin, preferably square or oblong, at least 4 cm (1½ inches) deep and about 14 × 11 cm (5½ × 4½ inches). Pour the mixture into this tin and stand on a flat surface to cool. When cold cut into 4-cm (1½-inch) cubes and serve either on a plate or in tiny paper cups, as used for sweets.

In Japan such jelly squares are often served with *shiso* leaves folded round them: large mint leaves may be used instead.

For an alternative style of presentation, pour a little of the warm mixture into a cup lined with a 20-cm (8-inch) square of cellophane or cling-wrap. Gather the edges together and tie with brightly coloured string, just above the red-bean jelly, to make little bags.

Fruit jelly (kingyokukan)

Makes about 700 ml (24 fl oz)

Jelly made with *agar-agar* is less rubbery than that made with gelatine and has a lower melting point. It can be flavoured with different fruit juices and decorated accordingly. Various flavourings and colours can be tried out, such as a slice of kiwi fruit on a lemon jelly, or a leaf of peppermint on a blackcurrant jelly. The jelly can be served in Paris goblets or other wine glasses, or it can be set in small oval dariole moulds and turned out on to a plate just before serving. It is eaten with a teaspoon. The flavour can be improved by chilling for a short time in the refrigerator; however, note that these cakes keep for only 2–3 days.

7 g (¼ oz) *agar-agar* or 1 stick Japanese *kanten*
300 g (11 oz) granulated sugar
15 ml (1 tablespoon) maltose (optional)

Alternative flavourings (for 350 ml/12 fl oz jelly):
30 ml (2 tablespoons) lemon juice
45 ml (3 tablespoons) raspberry juice
30 ml (2 tablespoons) Ribena
30 ml (2 tablespoons) concentrated orange juice + 15 ml (1 tablespoon) water
45 ml (3 tablespoons) crushed melon juice
45 ml (3 tablespoons) strained mango juice

Wash the *agar-agar* and soak for about 4 hours in cold water. If using Japanese *kanten* wrap in a clean cloth before soaking. Then squeeze out all the water and put the *agar-agar* in a pan with 500 ml (18 fl oz) cold water. Bring slowly to the boil over a moderate heat, then continue boiling gently, without stirring, until the *agar-agar* has dissolved (about 10 minutes). Add the sugar and stir over the heat until the sugar has dissolved. Strain the syrup through a cloth laid over a sieve and return the syrup to a clean pan. Squeeze the cloth to get out the last drops. Return to the heat and bring the temperature up to 93°C (200°F) (just below boiling). Hold at this temperature for 13 minutes. Remove from the heat and add the maltose; stir gently until dissolved. The jelly can now be flavoured to taste and poured into a mould to set. Unflavoured, it can be set in a square cake-tin, then cut into 1-cm (½-inch) cubes and mixed with an assortment of fruits poached in a sugar syrup, or a canned fruit salad.

Sweet potatoes and chestnuts

Serves 6–8

This is a traditional New Year sweet. Japanese housewives do not cook for the three days over the New Year holiday, and since this is also a time for visits from – and to – family and friends, many different foods, not all of them sweet, are prepared in advance. Many Japanese families keep a set of ornate lacquer New Year boxes, each divided into compartments, which they fill with various foods and offer to guests at this time.

300 g (10 oz) sweet potatoes
125 g (4 oz) whole chestnuts (canned in syrup), drained
60 ml (4 tablespoons) chestnut syrup (from the can)
45 ml (3 tablespoons) caster sugar
30 ml (2 tablespoons) *mirin*

Peel the potatoes thickly, cut into 3-cm (1-inch) slices and soak in cold water for 30 minutes. Afterwards put into clean water and boil until soft (about 20 minutes). Meanwhile cut the drained chestnuts into thirds. Mix the reserved syrup with 15 ml (1 tablespoon) sugar and the *mirin* and bring to the boil. Then leave on one side. When the potatoes are cooked, drain and dry over a low heat. Mix in 30 ml (2 tablespoons) sugar and rub through a fine sieve. Return to a clean pan and mix in the prepared syrup. Cook over a moderate heat, taking great care the mixture does not stick to the bottom of the pan and burn. If necessary add a little more water. When it is well heated through add the chestnut pieces and a few drops of water. Stir briskly over the heat for another 30 seconds, then turn out into a clean bowl. Keep covered in a cool place until required.

Ingredients

English names or descriptive translations for the different Japanese ingredients have been stated wherever possible throughout this book; Japanese names appear only where there is no alternative. In this chapter foods are referred to by both their English names (where these exist) and their Japanese *romaji* names. In the case of unfamiliar plants the Latin name is also included.

Seafoods

Agar-agar *(kanten)*, the vegetable form of gelatine, is a transparent, colourless dry seaweed sold, in Chinese grocers, in skeins that resemble crêpe knitting wool. It is also available from Japanese shops, in the form of either solid blocks or powder. It is used in sweets and needs soaking in water to soften before use.

Cod roe *(tarako)* is sold salted and, in the UK, deep-frozen. It is either grilled or served raw as a small dish for a main meal, or as a breakfast dish.

Fish paste *(kamaboko)* is a smooth, solid paste sold ready-cooked. It comes in several varieties and colours, including one on a wooden base. Available deep-frozen from Japanese shops in the UK, it has a limited freezer life. It can be sliced and used in one-pot dishes and in soups, or eaten just as it is in a salad, or used as a garnish.

Hanakatsuo (dried bonito fish flakes) is the fine shavings of hard-dried fillets of bonito, a fish of the same family as the mackerel. Used for making *dashi* (fish stock) and as a flavouring for foods and sauces, it is available from Japanese shops. Instant *dashi* is also available (see page 171).

Dried shrimps *(sakuraebi)* are used to give additional savoury flavouring to some dishes. More commonly used in Chinese than in Japanese cooking, they are available from Chinese grocers. Soak in hot water for 30 minutes before using.

Salted salmon steaks *(shiosake)* are eaten as a cold dish in a main meal, or for breakfast. They need no further preparation, though they may be grilled, and are as delicate in flavour as smoked salmon. They are available from Japanese shops.

Seaweed

Konbu (*kelp, Laminaria sp.*) comes in long dried strips. It has an iodine flavour and is used to flavour stocks and soups. It can be bought in either Japanese or Chinese grocers. The Chinese kelp (*hai ts'ao*), sometimes labelled 'dried tapeb seaweed', is coarser in flavour, so use half-quantities. *Konbu* quickly becomes very bitter if boiled rather than simmered.

Nori (laver, *Porphyra sp.*) is a seaweed which is highly processed in Japan into thin, dry, papery sheets 21 × 18 cm (8 × 6 inches). It is used for *sushi* rolls, eaten with rice particularly at breakfast, or served as a garnish. Best bought in Japanese shops, the Chinese variety used for soup is much less refined. To bring out the best flavour toast the shiny side for 4–5 seconds over a strong heat, taking great care not to burn it. After opening keep in an airtight container. *Nori* is also sold cut into thin strips or in small sheets for serving at table with rice.

Powdered green nori (*aonori ko*) is less a powder than minute shreds of green seaweed. Used as a garnish and flavouring, sometimes as a coating for fried fish, it is sold in jars in Japanese shops.

Wakame (no UK equivalent, *Undaria pinnatifida*) is a seaweed with long, thin fronds and a tough rim joining them together. Used for salads and soups, it is sold either salted or dried in Japanese shops. Soak either variety in cold water for 5 minutes. *Wakame* quickly becomes flaccid if overcooked so for soups cook for 1 minute only; for salads pour boiling water over to scald, then immediately refresh with cold water.

Fish

Fish in north Atlantic and British waters are always of different varieties, if not species, from those found in Japanese waters. Therefore it is always necessary to make substitutions when cooking Japanese in Britain. The fish listed below can, at least on occasion, be bought fresh in the UK and are suitable for Japanese cooking. Both fresh-water and sea fish are included.

Char Use whole for deep frying.

Dab Use whole for grilling, deep frying and simmering.

Eels Use filleted for grilling

Herrings Use whole for grilling and simmering.

Mackerel Use whole for grilling, filleted or sliced for baking and simmering.

Monkfish Use sliced for deep frying.

Octopus Use tentacles for vinegared appetizer.

Plaice Use filleted for deep frying.

Red mullet Use whole (if really fresh) for grilling.

Salmon and sea trout Use filleted or sliced for *sashimi*, grilling, soup and one-pot dishes.

Sea bass Use filleted for grilling and sliced for soups; if really fresh, use filleted for *sashimi*.

Sea bream Use whole for grilling, sliced for soups.

Sole Use whole for grilling, filleted for deep frying.

Sprats Use whole for grilling and simmering.

Squid Use sliced for deep frying, grilling and salads, whole for simmering.

Trout Use whole for grilling, filleted for *sashimi*.

Tunny Use filleted for *sashimi* if fresh and in some soups when frozen. This is sold in Japanese shops.

Live cockles and mussels (increasingly hard to find) can be used in soups in their shells.

Boiled crabs If fresh use in salads and other dishes.

Raw, uncooked prawns or shrimps These may not be sold in the UK in their natural state. The raw, grey-coloured prawns on sale have always been frozen and are imported. Pink prawns, either frozen or unfrozen, have always been boiled.

FROZEN FISH sold in the UK and suitable for some Japanese dishes include:

Cod Use as steaks for grilling, filleted for simmering and one-pot dishes.

Haddock Use in place of cod.

Sardines Use whole for grilling and simmering.

Fruit and nuts

Chestnuts (*kuri*) are similar to the European chestnut and are used in various sweet dishes. Peel fresh chestnuts by making an incision in the top of the shell and putting them in boiling water for 5 minutes.

Ginko nuts (*ginnan*) are the fleshy nuts of the *Ginko bilboa* tree, sold fresh in Japan. In the UK canned nuts from China, called 'white nuts', can be bought. Used in one-pot dishes in Japan, canned nuts have little flavour compared with fresh nuts.

Pickled sour plums (*umeboshi*) are the pickled fruit of the Japanese apricot (*Prunus mume*), which has a very sour, dry flavour. They are used for flavouring rice and other foods. They can be bought in cartons from Japanese grocers, or in jars labelled 'preserved sour plums in brine' from Chinese grocers. Both varieties keep well.

Poppy seeds (*keshinomi*) are used either as a garnish or as an ingredient in seven-spice pepper. They are available from healthfood stores and Indian grocers. Toast in the same manner as sesame seeds.

Sesame seeds (*goma*) come in both white and black varieties. White sesame seeds can be bought in their natural state from Indian, Chinese and Japanese stores, or ready-toasted and crushed in Japanese shops. To toast white sesame seeds put them in a dry pan over a medium heat until they start to turn golden brown (3–4 minutes, stirring with a wooden spoon all the time). Take great care they do not burn, even after taking them from the heat. Grind using either a pestle and mortar or a rolling-pin on a board. Use as a garnish or as a flavouring for sauces. Chinese sesame paste or Greek *tahina* may be substituted for ground toasted sesame seeds, but the flavour is much inferior to that of freshly toasted seeds. Black sesame seeds, either toasted or raw, can be bought in Japanese shops.

Yuzu (no English name) is a citrus fruit (from *Citrus junos*) with a bitter, rather dry flesh and a fragrant rind. It is used as a flavouring or garnish or in some savoury sauces. It is sold frozen in Japanese grocers. Use lemon or Seville orange peel as a substitute.

Beans and farinaceous foods

Adzuki beans (*azuki*) are small red beans used for making red rice, a traditional festival dish in Japan, and also for the sweet bean-paste used for filling various cakes. They are sold in healthfood stores and Chinese grocers. Soak for 1 hour before cooking.

Soya beans (*daizu*) are round, cream-coloured dried beans sold in healthfood stores and Chinese grocers. Not often eaten unprocessed, they require soaking for 12 hours before use.

Beancurd (*tofu*) is made from soya beans (see above), and when fresh has a delicate, slightly nutty flavour. There are two basic kinds of beancurd in Japan: cotton beancurd (*momen tofu*), which is a firm pressed variety used for frying and simmering, and silk beancurd (*kinugoshi*), of a delicate, junket-like consistency, which is used mainly in soups. Japanese cotton beancurd is made commercially in England and can now be bought in sealed packets in some healthfood shops. Imported long-life silk beancurd from Japan can be bought ready-made in a packet from many Chinese grocers and healthfood shops. It is rather tasteless but the texture is good for soups. House Tofu and Towfu are silk beancurd mixes sold in many Chinese, Japanese and healthfood stores, with English instructions, and are not difficult to make successfully.

Commercially-made Chinese beancurd in the UK lies between the two varieties in consistency. It is sold by Chinese grocers in square cakes of various sizes, and can be converted into cotton beancurd by wrapping it tightly in a towel and pressing between two plates for about 4 hours. To store beancurd, empty it at once from the polythene bag in which it is sold and immerse in a bowl of cold water. Keep in a cool place and change the water each day. Beancurd kept in this way will stay fresh for about 5 days.

Freeze-dried beancurd (*koya tofu*) is sold in small flat cakes in Japanese grocers and some healthfood shops. Soak in warm water for about 10 minutes: the cakes will soften and swell until they resemble small squares of sponge. A packet will keep for several months.

Aburage are deep-fried flat cakes of beancurd which can be bought in Japanese grocers in the UK and will keep for a short period of time in a freezer without deteriorating. They quickly go bad if kept in the refrigerator.

Natto are sticky fermented soya beans with a slight flavour of decay – not to everyone's taste. They are eaten with rice and a raw egg for breakfast or used as a flavouring for salad dressings. They can be bought frozen in small packets from Japanese grocers.

Miso (fermented bean-paste) is a highly nutritious soft bean-paste made by fermenting soya beans with rice or other grains. It comes in different colours and flavours depending on the variety, but basically there are two main types: 'white' is made with a rice mould and is sweeter than 'red', which is made with a barley mould and is darker and saltier than the white.

Kome miso is a variety of white *miso* sold in some healthfood shops in the UK. *Mugi miso* is the normal red *miso* sold in healthfood shops, although there is also a lighter version called *genmai miso*. *Hatcho miso*, made only with soya beans, is a dark, solid *miso* with a strong, salty flavour suitable for soups. (Different varieties with other names appear in Japanese shops, where the assistants will gladly provide guidance.)

Miso will keep for a very long time in the refrigerator. Although it was an ancient Chinese sauce, it is not used in modern Chinese cookery and therefore cannot be bought in Chinese grocers.

Rice (*kome*) in Japan is a short-grained variety which is sticky when cooked. Buy American Rose short-grained rice in Japanese and some Chinese grocers (*not* the Italian pudding rice generally sold in supermarkets). Chinese or patna long-grained rice may be used for plain boiled rice with a Japanese meal but it is not suitable for *sushi* or vinegared-rice dishes.

Glutinous rice (*mochi gome*) is a round-grained variety of rice with a high gluten content which cooks to a very sticky consistency. It is used in Japan for red rice and other sweet dishes as well as for wine-making, and it is sold in Chinese and Japanese shops. It needs soaking for 1 hour before cooking.

Rice noodles (*harusame*) are near-transparent white noodles made from rice or potato flour. They are used dry as a coating for deep-fried *tempura*, or in Japanese one-pot dishes, for which they should be softened in hot water before use. Sold in Chinese and Japanese grocers, they are sometimes called 'spring rain' in Japanese cookery.

Buckwheat noodles (*soba*) are slightly greyish noodles with a distinctive peppery flavour. They are available dried, in packets, from healthfood stores as well as from Japanese grocers. There is also a green *soba* flavoured with tea, called *cha soba*.

Wheat noodles (*udon*) are round or flat very white noodles made from wheat flour with no egg in them. They are sold in packets. *Somen* and *hiyamugi* are different qualities of very thin white wheat noodles; *hiyamugi* in particular are used for cold noodle dishes.

Gluten (*fu*) is the protein remaining in wheat flour after the starch has been washed out. In Japan this is dried into flat cakes or round beads and used in soups and one-pot dishes. Only the flat cakes can be bought in the UK, from Japanese shops. Soak for 10 minutes in warm water before using.

Kudzu (*kuzu ko*) is a delicate flour, made from the root of *Pueraria lobata*, used for thickening sauces and particularly for a dry starch coating for fried foods. It is sold in Japanese grocers. Arrowroot may be used as a substitute.

Potato flour (*katakuriko*) is used for thickening sauces and is available from Chinese grocers. It should be added to sauces at a temperature well below boiling point and stirred in carefully – to avoid a rubbery lump at the bottom of the pan. It produces a much clearer sauce than the ubiquitous cornflour, which may be used as a substitute. Use also as a dry coating for fried foods.

Commercially prepared sauces, seasonings and spices

Soy sauce (*shoyu*) is made from soya beans by a process of hydrolysis. Japanese soy sauces are thinner and lighter than Chinese ones. Buy a variety labelled 'naturally brewed', such as Kikkoman, if buying Japanese soy sauce, or substitute *light* soy sauce from China. (Light soy sauces are saltier and lighter in flavour than dark ones.)

Vinegar (*su*) in Japan is white and made from rice. It has a light, delicate taste, and is much preferable to the heavily acidulated malt vinegars of the West, which should never be used as a substitute. It is sold in both Japanese and Chinese grocers. As a substitute use cider vinegar diluted to half strength with vinegar.

Sake (fortified rice wine) is more refined and has less flavour than Chinese rice wine (*shaoxing*), which is also used for cooking. Dry sherry is not a satisfactory substitute since its flavour is too strong, but vodka and water (half and half) are a possible alternative. *Sake* is sold in Chinese, Japanese and some wine stores. For drinking, *sake* should be warmed to blood heat by standing the container in hot water and served in small carafes.

Mirin is a specially brewed sweetened rice wine with an almost syrupy consistency, used only in cooking. It is sold in Japanese grocers. Use either half caster sugar, half water or 1 caster sugar to half water and half vodka as a substitute.

Dashi (fish stock) may be bought in its 'instant' form, in packets, from Japanese stores and some Chinese grocers. Instant *dashi* saves time and provides a very acceptable Japanese-type stock-base for cooking and soups.

Sesame oil (*goma abura*) is the oil extracted from sesame seeds. It has a delicate flavour and will not withstand high temperatures. It is sold in both Japanese and Chinese grocers in the UK.

Wasabi mustard Often called Japanese horseradish, this is not to be confused with either Japanese or English mustard; it is a hot, fragrant green paste made from the powdered root of an acquatic plant, *Wasabia japonica*. It can be bought ready-made in tubes or as a powder in tins from Japanese grocers. Make up the powder afresh when required with a little water, like English mustard. Ready-made *wasabi* must be refrigerated after opening and does not keep its flavour long.

Seven-spice pepper (*shichimi*), sometimes also called *shichimi togarashi*, is a spicy mixture of chilli pepper, black pepper, sesame seeds, poppy seeds, hemp, dried zest of orange, powdered *nori*, white pepper and *sansho* pepper. The choice and mixture of spices vary. Seven-spice pepper is sold in Japanese grocers.

Chilli pepper (*ichimi* or *togarashi*), sometimes called one-spice pepper, is sold either as minute flakes or dried red chillis or as straight cayenne pepper. Finely chopped dried chillis may be used as a substitute.

Sansho pepper (*kona zansho*) is a pungent, rather sour, coarse powder made from the ground seed-pods of the prickly ash, *Zanthoxylum piperitum*. Sold in Japanese grocers, it is used mainly as a seasoning for fried or grilled foods.

Vegetables and vegetable products

Aubergines (*nasu*) in Japan are about one-quarter the size of the aubergines commonly sold in UK markets. However, smaller varieties can now often be found in Indian shops.

Bamboo shoots (*takenoko*) are sold canned in Chinese and Japanese grocers. Once opened, bamboo shoots may be kept for up to 10 days by boiling every 2–3 days in fresh water and storing in a clean container in the refrigerator.

Black fungus (*kikurage*) is a variety of *Auriculariales*, an edible fungus which grows on trees. It has a delicate, smoky flavour and a crunchy texture, and it resembles black dried leaves. It can be bought in Chinese and Japanese shops, and must be soaked in warm water for 30 minutes, then washed, before use. As it is too light to weigh, quantities in the recipes have been stated by volume.

Burdock (*gobe*) is the long root of *Arctium lappa*, a member of the daisy family which grows wild in Britain and is cultivated in Japan, where the root is eaten as a vegetable. It is sold in cans, and sometimes fresh, in Japanese grocers. Scorzonera or salsify, both also members of the *Compositae* family, may be substituted. When using any of these vegetables fresh, peel, then place immediately in acidulated water (600 ml/1 pint water plus the juice of half a lemon, or the same quantity of vinegar) to prevent them from turning black.

Chrysanthemum (*shungiku*) is the edible *Chrysanthemum coronarium*. Both the yellow flowers and the young leaves, which have a pleasing flavour and a texture and colour resembling spinach, may be eaten. Spinach may be substituted for the leaves. They are not a commercial vegetable in the UK but it is possible to buy seeds from Thompson and Morgan (Seed Merchants), Ipswich, Norfolk which are very easy to grow.

Cucumbers (*kyuri*) in Japan are about one-third the size of the cucumbers sold in the UK. Western cucumbers should therefore be cut in half lengthways before being cut into the right shape or size for a Japanese salad.

Leek (*negi*) The Japanese use a long white onion which is not available in the UK. Young leeks are often the closest substitute, but the very large spring onions sometimes sold in supermarkets are also suitable for Japanese cooking. The thin spring onions sold for salads in the UK and often used in Chinese cooking are not suitable.

Lotus root (*renkon*) is the rhizome of the water-lily *Nelumbium speciosum*, and is sold canned or, very occasionally, fresh, in Chinese grocers in the UK. In Japanese cooking it is used in simmered dishes, or, if fresh, deep-fried as a crunchy vegetable in *tempura*. To keep canned lotus root, once opened, boil in clean water every two days and store in a clean container in a cool place. It keeps for about two weeks.

Dried mushrooms (*hoshi shiitake*) In Japan these mushrooms, *Lentinus edodes*, are sold fresh, but in the UK only the expensive dried variety is available, from both Chinese and Japanese stores. Always soak in warm water for 30 minutes and remove the hard stalk before use. The soaking water can be used in stocks.

Shiso (beefsteak plant) is a small herb with bright green leaves, *Perilla ocimoides* or *Perilla nankinensis*. It has a sharp, slightly minty flavour. The leaves can be bought fresh from Japanese grocers, but are expensive. It is used for *tempura* and as a garnish. Seeds of this plant can be bought from Thomas Butcher Ltd, The Garden Centre, 60 Wickham Road, Shirley, Croydon, Surrey (01–654 3720).

Snow peas (*kinusaya*), also called sugar peas, are flat green pea-pods that are eaten whole. They are more commonly available during the winter in the UK, particularly from Chinese grocers, but can be grown successfully in the garden during the summer; the seeds are sold by most good seedsmen.

Sweet potatoes (*satsuma imo*), *Ipomoea batatas*, are now sold widely in the UK. Choose the purple-skinned variety for preference.

White radish (*daikon*), also sold in the UK as Dutch rettish, looks like a giant white carrot and is known as *mooli* in many Indian stores. It is widely available in UK markets.

Yams (*ko imo*), *Dioscorea batatas*, are small, scaly, slightly fibrous-skinned root vegetables sold in Indian, West Indian and sometimes Chinese stores. They are called edoes in UK West Indian markets.

Konnyaku (devil's-tongue jelly) is a solid, jelly-like cake made from the flesh of *Amorphallus konjac*, a sub-species of the sweet potato. It is sold in packets in Japanese shops and used mainly in simmered and one-pot dishes. It will keep for about 2 weeks after being opened, provided it is put into fresh cold water every day. Before use, boil in plenty of unsalted water for about 3 minutes, then dry in a dry pan over a moderate heat.

Shiritaki is a jelly processed from the same plant (*Amorphallus konjac*), but in the form of thin white threads rather like noodles. It is used in one-pot dishes, particularly *sukiyaki*, and is sold in packets and cans. It will keep for about 3 days after being opened. Before use, boil in plenty of unsalted water for 3 minutes, then drain.

Pickles (*tsukemono*) Many kinds of commercially prepared pickles are on sale in Japanese grocers in the UK. Among them are those made with cucumbers, aubergines, *shiso* buds and ginger threads. They are usually sold in plastic packets and are not expensive. They keep well in the refrigerator when opened, so it is well worth keeping several packets of different flavours to suit different tastes.

Winter melon strips (*kampyo*) are thin, dried strips of winter melon used for tying various 'rolled' foods. Rub with salt and boil for 10 minutes in clean water before use. Japanese winter melon strips are highly processed and bleached; Chinese winter melon strips are not bleached and should only be soaked in hot water until soft.

Japanese teas

Bancha is the coarsest grade of Japanese green tea, often served in restaurants before the meal, and most commonly drunk throughout the day at home. Make it with not-quite-boiling water and allow to infuse for no more than 2 minutes, otherwise it will become bitter.

Sencha is a finer grade of green tea, more expensive than *bancha*. Make with hot, not boiling, water, and allow to infuse for no more than 2 minutes. Serve in small cups after meals. In Japan this tea is made in tiny earthenware pots.

Matcha is the green powdered tea used in the tea ceremony. It is made by the cup and whisked into a froth. A small, sweet cake is usually served with it.

Miscellaneous

Quails' eggs (*uzurano-tamago*) are used hard-boiled in soups and one-pot dishes. They can be bought fresh or canned in Chinese grocers and hard-boiled in some delicatessens.

Rice crackers are small, savoury biscuits made with rice flour and flavoured with *nori* and/or sesame seeds. They are highly glazed with sugar and soy sauce. Sold in small packets in both Chinese and Japanese grocers, they make a good accompaniment to pre-dinner drinks.

Maltose (*mizuame*) is a semi-solid syrup extracted from wheat or other grains. It is not sweet like sucrose but contributes to the texture of a dish. It can be bought in Chinese grocers in the UK.

Index